Contesting a Will
without a Lawyer
The DIY guide for Canadians

Lynne Butler, LAWYER

Self-Counsel Press
(a division of)
International Self-Counsel Press Ltd.
Canada   USA

Self-Counsel Press acknowledges the financial support of the Government of Canada for our publishing activities. **Canadä**

Printed in Canada.

First edition: 2018

Library and Archives Canada Cataloguing in Publication

Butler, Lynne, author
  Contesting a will without a lawyer : the DIY guide for Canadians / Lynne Butler.
  (Legal series)

Issued in print and electronic formats.

ISBN 978-1-77040-305-5 (softcover).—ISBN 978-1-77040-498-4 (EPUB).—
ISBN 978-1-77040-499-1 (Kindle)

  1. Wills—Canada—Popular works. 2. Probate law and practice—Canada—Popular works.
I. Title. II. Series: Self-Counsel legal series

| KE808.B88 2018 | 346.7105'4 | C2018-904033-5 |
| KF755.B88 2018 | | C2018-904034-3 |

Self-Counsel Press
(a division of)
International Self-Counsel Press Ltd.

Bellingham, WA
USA

North Vancouver, BC
Canada

Contents

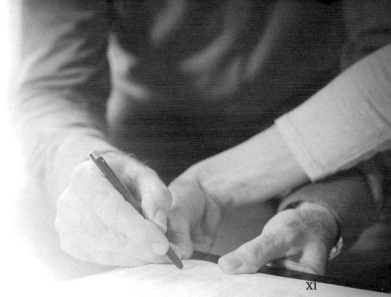

Checklist

Samples

Tables

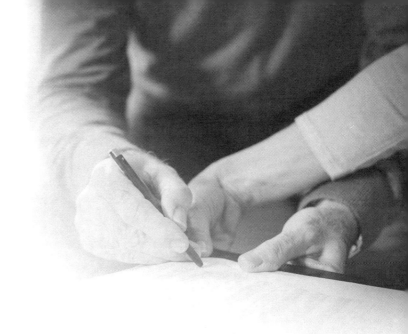

Notice to Readers

Laws are constantly changing. Every effort is made to keep this publication as current as possible. However, the author, the publisher, and the vendor of this book make no representations or warranties regarding the outcome or the use to which the information in this book is put and are not assuming any liability for any claims, losses, or damages arising out of the use of this book. The reader should not rely on the author or the publisher of this book for any professional advice. Please be sure that you have the most recent edition.

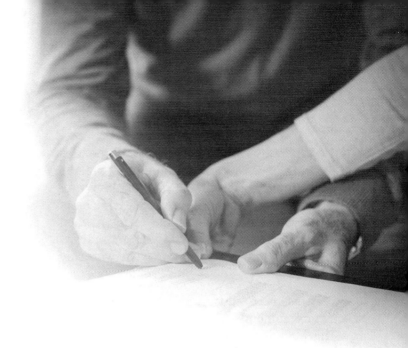

Introduction

There are hundreds of ways in which the estate of a deceased person can end up in a fight. Sometimes a complex legal issue comes up and can only be resolved by a judge. In other cases it's a matter of people not being able to settle specific but important issues. Despite there being so many ways for estates to fall apart, there are not many ways to resolve the disputes. There is no government estate department or agency whose job it is to ensure that estates run properly. Many estate disputes end up in court.

The purpose of this book is two-fold. One is to inform you about the types of lawsuits that touch on estates and what is involved in each of them, to help you decide whether or not you want to begin the process of suing someone due to an estate dispute. Starting a lawsuit is a serious matter and you need to think it through with the facts at hand. The other purpose is, for those who decide to go ahead with litigation, to help you navigate the paperwork and the courts.

In this book, I do not encourage people to sue each other, nor do I attempt to talk anyone out of it. Estate litigation is an enormous undertaking that is not to be taken lightly. It's expensive, time consuming, and often ugly. However, I fully understand that sometimes it is necessary or advisable to sue an estate or contest a will.

In this book, I strive to be straightforward and factual. I was first called to the bar 31 years ago and have always practiced in the area of wills and estates. I have handled many estate lawsuits in that time and I hope to lend my experience to those of you who are working on such cases without a lawyer. Even those of you who are working with lawyers will find this book useful as it will explain things that your lawyer won't have the time to explain. It will show you samples of the documents used in such cases with explanations of why those documents are being prepared. This should help you save a great deal on your legal fees as you will be better prepared for your meetings with your lawyer and will use less of his or her time.

While there will be discussion of the idea of suing an estate that is intended to guide you through a sensible decision-making process, this book will also provide specific help. There will be samples of the forms needed in each province and territory to get matters into court, and checklists to ensure you stay on track.

This book does not cover defending against someone who is contesting an estate. This book is about launching the lawsuit and how to approach the various steps you will need to take to move your lawsuit through the legal system. However, the information in this book will be helpful to anyone, either launching a lawsuit or defending one, to understand the legal process and to anticipate next steps.

In this book, I don't include information about estates in Quebec. This is because all provinces and territories in Canada use a common-law legal system except for Quebec, which has a civil code. Quebec's laws, processes, and forms are all very different from those in the rest of the country.

1
The Why: Pros and Cons of Suing an Estate

Before getting started on a lawsuit, read this section about the upside and the downside of starting litigation. What is it that you want from the will challenge? What can you expect to achieve, and what will it cost you in terms of time, money, and emotional strain to reach that goal? Be realistic about your situation, your motivation, and your prospects for a positive outcome. Though estate litigation is among the most emotional litigation you will ever experience, do your best to take the emotion out of the equation and look at the situation as objectively as you can.

In this chapter, you will find some of the most often-heard reasons that people commence lawsuits against estates. Some of them will apply to you and some will not. You will also find a list of what many people find to be the downside of estate litigation. Again, many will apply to you. We are discussing these topics here to help you clarify what you can expect from suing an estate and decide whether it is the best way for you to go.

1. Potential Upsides of Suing an Estate

1.1 Principles

Many people feel that whatever has happened to derail an estate is the result of someone acting in a way that is selfish, greedy, or even criminal. They believe that they cannot live with themselves if they do not attempt to right the wrong that has been done. Often litigants will say that even if they lose the case, they will have done all they can to put things right. In other words, they are not trying to gain financially; they are trying to stop someone from taking something that does not belong to him or her or from acting in a way that should not be tolerated. They have to act according to their conscience.

For example, an executor might take charge of an estate but then not distribute the estate for years. The executor moves into the deceased's home without paying rent, drives the deceased's car, and won't tell anyone what's happening with the estate. After months or even years of this, the beneficiaries get fed up and want the executor to stop abusing the estate. At that point, the beneficiaries just want the executor to be fair and to give answers. Cases like this are not usually about whether the beneficiaries get anything themselves — or at least are not just about that — but are about forcing the executor to do the job he or she is supposed to be doing.

In cases like this, whether it is the executor or a beneficiary or some other party who is acting improperly, it gives the other parties closure and peace if they personally take steps that result in a positive outcome.

1.2 Stopping abuse or fraud

There are tens of thousands of cases in our country of adult children taking advantage of aging parents and grandparents. This affects estates because the abuse often takes the form of joint bank accounts, names added to property, or wills changed to favour someone in a position of influence. Many of these cases, sadly, go undetected. Even some of those that are discovered are let go because other family members don't know what to do about it or can't afford to do anything to put a stop to it. For those who do choose to challenge an estate where there appears to have been elder financial abuse, there is immense satisfaction in stopping the fraudulent person from doing further damage.

1.3 Carrying out the wishes of the deceased

Many a lawsuit is launched against an executor who is not carrying out the instructions left in the will. It is a more common cause of estate litigation than most people realize. This is partly because a startling number of executors work on estates with no guidance whatsoever and are doing things incorrectly. Most people who take on the role of executor have never done so before and are not familiar with how wills work. They think they know what they are doing and believe they are acting in good faith, but they make mistakes that they refuse to correct. There are also dishonest and greedy executors who use the estate as their personal windfall, but they are not the majority.

The impetus behind the legal challenge in these cases is simply to ensure that the executor carries out the will as the deceased instructed and not as the executor personally chooses as a perceived better or fairer arrangement.

1.4 Financial support

When certain family members such as certain types of dependants are left out of a will or are given only a small gift from the estate, they may contest the will to gain a larger share of the estate, as discussed in Chapter 3. The upside of estate litigation in those cases is that the beneficiary may receive financial support that is crucial to his or her lifestyle and in fact may be his or her only financial resource. Had the person not sued the estate, he or she would have nothing to live on.

1.5 Closure

There is a lot to be said for finally having an upsetting, distracting issue settled once and for all. By the time a lawsuit winds to an end, everyone is happy for it to be over.

2. Potential Downsides of Suing an Estate

2.1 Length of time

If an estate issue goes all the way to trial, you can expect it to take up to five years to wrap up everything. That five years is not a waiting period by any means; during that time you would participate in some combination of trial-related activities that might include filing paperwork, motions before the court, cross-examinations (also called discoveries or depositions), case management sessions, mediation, settlement discussions, witness preparation, finding expert witnesses, and eventually the trial itself.

The vast majority of disputes do not make it all the way to trial. Most are settled one way or the other before reaching that stage. A settlement can be proposed by either side at any time. In such case, it would likely not take five years to conclude matters, but it could still take one or two years. Alternatives to carrying out a lawsuit are discussed in Chapter 14.

Before starting a lawsuit, be aware that it will be a part of your life for a long time. You will likely end up taking time off work or other activities. If you are not working with a lawyer, you can expect the lawsuit to take longer simply because you will make mistakes that lead to delays and adjournments.

2.2 Cost

Lawsuits can be horribly expensive if they drag on for a long time. Many readers of this book are considering launching a lawsuit without using a lawyer while others are working with lawyers but are referring to this book for additional information. I will look at both situations in this section.

If you have hired a lawyer to conduct the lawsuit for you and the matter goes all the way to a trial, you should expect to pay tens of thousands of dollars. In 2016, *Canadian Lawyer* magazine took a survey of legal fees charged by lawyers for trials across Canada and published the results. The average legal fee for a seven-day trial was $86,000. Because this is an average, you can assume that some trials cost less and others cost more. As mentioned in the previous section, holding a trial includes a lot of preliminary steps so presumably this price quoted by *Canadian Lawyer* magazine includes the fees for those steps. Keep in mind that this number is for legal fees only; it does not include court fees, witness fees, expert fees, accounting fees, or other similar disbursements you might need to make.

Most lawyers charge an hourly fee for their services. You will find that the contingency fee — the kind where the lawyer charges a percentage of the amount won — is almost never used in estate litigation. Most estate-related lawsuits simply don't lend themselves well to that type of arrangement.

Traditionally, the lawyers involved in estate litigation were paid out of the estate. Those days are gone. Today, not many lawsuits are funded by the estate itself, so costs must always be factored in if you are considering suing. For a thorough discussion about legal costs, see Chapter 13.

High legal fees are one of the main reasons that individuals decide to try to sue on their own without legal help. If you are considering doing so, please realize that you must be completely committed to the lawsuit and all that it entails. While you may not have to pay legal fees, you may still have to pay probate fees, court fees, witness fees, filing fees, and expenses such as photocopying and printing.

2.3 Stress on you and your immediate family

Hopefully your spouse or partner is supportive of your involvement in the lawsuit. With some good luck and some sensible management, you may be able to keep the impact of the lawsuit to a minimum. That's not always the case, particularly if family finances are involved.

2.4 Damage to family relationships

Most of the time, the people who are being sued on an estate or who are opposing each other on a dispute are family members, often even siblings. This results in family relationships being so badly damaged that they can never be repaired. You will likely find it impossible to share a Christmas dinner or a summer picnic with someone who has just finished suggesting in court that you are a greedy liar.

The emotions experienced by individuals involved in estate litigation are intense and varied. At the beginning, there is usually some shock and disbelief at what is happening and dismay that the dispute cannot be amicably resolved. This tends to harden into anger and resentment as people become entrenched in their opposing positions. As time goes by, the anger deepens and frustration begins to tinge everything. There may be shame at the way family members are behaving, or embarrassment because of the airing of family matters that should be private. There is also a profound sense of loss and grief since you will have lost not just the person who passed away but also the family members who are on the opposite side of the dispute.

Even family members who are not directly involved will probably take sides. Often clients tell me that it is not the lawsuit that created the damage, but the underlying action taken by someone that caused the need for a lawsuit. However you see this, and no matter where you stand in the family circle, be aware that it will be a monumental disruption for your extended family.

2.5 A steep learning curve

As you will find as you go through this book, there is an enormous amount of information that you must digest and work with. Conducting your own lawsuit will be like taking a crash course in litigation. Even if you are working with a lawyer, it can be tough to understand the vocabulary, the procedures, and the reasons why certain parties can and cannot do certain steps.

2.6 There might be less than you think in the estate

It's possible to begin a lawsuit against an estate only to find that it is valued at much less than you thought. The reasons for this might be that legal costs are eating up the estate, that property values have dropped, or that the deceased had a lot of debt. It could also be that by the time you brought your lawsuit, the executor had already distributed a large part of the estate to the beneficiaries. If that was done before you launched your lawsuit and the executor was following the will, you likely will have no recourse towards the part of the estate that has already been distributed.

3. What Is Your Motivation?

Before reading the rest of this chapter, I suggest that you take a moment to do something that you will find very useful. Pretend for a moment that you have walked into a lawyer's office and you want to tell the lawyer in one brief sentence what you want him or her to do about your dispute. Don't worry about the facts and details right now; assume that the lawyer knows who has passed away and what has happened. Just state in one brief question or statement what you want to do about it. Once you've done that, read on.

Was your initial, one-sentence statement something like these?

- I'm furious with him or her for doing this.

- Can I call the police on the executor?

- There's no way I'm putting up with this crap.

- I don't care what it costs, I'm putting a stop to him or her.

- I want you to make him or her sorry he or she ever crossed me.

Or, was your initial statement more like this?

- Should I be contesting this or leaving it alone?

- How can this be resolved?

- Do I really need to drag this thing through the courts?

- It's not about the money; it's about following someone's wishes.

The point of going through this exercise is for you to see more clearly what your motivation really is for wanting to challenge the estate. It is essential that you understand your motives and use that awareness to clarify your overall goals. Though you may not realize it at first, your initial statements and questions are very revealing about what you really want from the lawsuit and how things are going to go for you during the course of disputing the estate.

For example, let's say that one of your siblings had been helping himself to some of your aging mother's money before your mother passed away. Nobody knew that your brother was taking money from her until she was deceased and her bank accounts showed just how much they were depleted. How do you feel about the situation? You'll probably find that your emotions run the spectrum from fury with the brother to guilt about not

protecting your mother to sadness about the current situation.

Now channel those emotions into what you'd like to see happen. What is your number one goal? Is it to have the money replaced so that your mother's wishes can be carried out? Or is it a burning desire to punish your brother for what he did? Do you want the world to know the story so that everyone around him will feel contempt for him? Or would you just like to get everything quietly back on track and distribute your mother's estate?

Your motivations and goals are absolutely essential to the question of whether you should contest the will. If what you want is just to get things back on track and replace the money, there may well be another way to attain the goal. Mediation might work, or perhaps there is a way for the executor of the estate to negotiate some kind of settlement. Creative solutions can often be found if everyone stays calm and focused.

If, on the other hand, your goal is to punish and embarrass your brother, you need to take some time to ponder whether using the courts is really the best way to go. Suing someone will not make you feel better. The court won't act as a hammer for you to hit someone. Taking court action out of spite will bounce back on you eventually.

When you are driven by emotion your judgment is off and your decisions will reflect that. You will be disappointed with the results of the lawsuit no matter what happens because you are expecting something that the courts can't deliver.

4. Conflicts of Interest

In estate matters, family members often have more than one role. For example, a child of the deceased might be named as the executor of the will as well as one of the beneficiaries of the estate. Normally this is not a problem, as it is legal and workable for a person to be all of those things.

However, the multiple roles become problematic when what works best for the person in one role is not the same as what works best for him or her in another role. You cannot attack the will and defend the will at the same time. This is known as a conflict of interest. This is something you must consider carefully if you are considering suing an estate but you are named as the executor of the estate.

The conflict arises because suing an estate when you are the executor is just like taking both sides in an argument. You cannot fully commit to the battle on both sides of it and you would end up letting down one side. This is just common sense. An executor's primary task is to follow the will while doing everything he or she can to protect and maximize the estate. If you were, for example, suing the estate as the wife of the deceased, asking for a greater share than the will gives you, it is simply impossible for you also to act as the executor who is upholding the will.

This does not mean that a person who is named as an executor is forever barred from asking the court for assistance in changing the estate. Far from it. But it does mean that you will have to give up the job of executor if you choose to sue the estate. If you tried to contest the will while continuing on in your role as executor, you would find that the other people involved in the issue would not stand for it, nor would the judge be likely to stand for it.

5. Deadlines for Starting Your Lawsuit

There are a number of time limits or limitation dates that apply in estate situations, depending on the facts of your case. If you are a spouse who wants to claim a greater share of the estate, the time limit in most places is six months from the time probate or administration is granted. In Ontario, the time limit is six months from the time the person died. In British Columbia, a person who wants to apply for variation of a will must apply within 180 days of the date of death. Since this is such a short time period in every jurisdiction, it is a good idea to get started on that claim as soon as possible.

Note that the deadlines mentioned above are specifically for the kind of challenge known as dependant's relief, as discussed in Chapter 3. As a general rule, individuals who wish to contest a will on the usual grounds such as undue influence or lack of mental capacity must begin their lawsuit within two years of the death of the testator. Grounds for contesting a will are discussed in Chapter 2.

6. Before You Start a Lawsuit, Consider a Demand Letter

Every lawsuit should be preceded by a demand letter. This is a letter to the person you intend to sue that tells him or her what you are going to sue about and gives you both a chance to settle it before you go to court. The letter is intended to accomplish a few goals, all of which may help you resolve your dispute.

A demand letter opens the discussion. In your letter, you will explain to the recipient what he or she has done wrong, and why his or her actions are in contravention of the law. You will explain how it affects your legal rights. A demand letter also includes your statement of how you want the matter to be resolved. You tell the person you're suing (the defendant) what you want. For example, you might say that you intend to ask the court to remove him or her as executor. You might say that you intend to contest the validity of the will. Once you've said what the issue is, you go further and say what would satisfy you in terms of settlement. For example, you might say that you believe you are entitled to $50,000 from the estate. You might say that the joint bank account should be shared among all of the deceased's children. Obviously these are just examples and the specific content will depend on the facts of your case.

Sometimes the demand letter results in a willingness by the other person to discuss the issue and try to settle. Perhaps there will be no need to resort to the court at all and by writing a letter you will have saved months or years of litigation. In other cases, the demand letter elicits a response that makes it perfectly clear that the person you want to sue is more than willing to battle it out in court. At least you will know where you stand.

A demand letter is more formal than most letters you would write. It can be very difficult to stay on track because it is tempting to use the letter to insult or blame the other person, or to vent your frustrations. None of that is appropriate, nor will it do anything but aggravate and inflame the other person. Your letter should be businesslike, calm, organized, polite, firm, and straightforward. It must stay on point and not include insults or threats.

Sample 1 is a demand letter that will demonstrate the sort of language you should use, and shows the various components of an effective letter.

Here are some tips to build an effective demand letter:

1. Make sure you send it to the right person.

2. Mark it "without prejudice."

3. Indicate on the letter the method of delivery you will use.

4. State why you are writing the letter.

5. Describe the problem or issue.

6. Tell the person what you want.

7. Indicate what steps you'll take if settlement isn't reached.

8. Set a time limit for the person to respond to your letter.

SAMPLE 1
DEMAND LETTER

October 10, 2019

WITHOUT PREJUDICE

Delivered by courier

Joseph Wickham
125 Maple Street
Canadian City, ON
A1A 1A1

Dear Mr. Wickham,

Re: The Estate of Jeanne Amherst

This letter is written to you as the executor of the estate of Jeanne Amherst. As you are aware, I am a residuary beneficiary of the estate and as such I am entitled to a share of the household and personal belongings of Mrs. Amherst.

It has come to my attention that you have distributed personal possessions including jewellery and a vehicle from the estate to people who are not beneficiaries under the will. I understand that you have given some of Mrs. Amherst's jewellery to your daughter and you have given Mrs. Amherst's car to your son. By delivering these items to these people you have breached your duty to the estate.

As executor, your responsibility is to distribute the items according to the will. The items in the estate belong to the beneficiaries and you have no legal right to give the items to anyone else. Despite my verbal request that you reverse these gifts, you have not done so.

If these items are not returned to the estate within 14 days of the date of this letter, I will have no choice but to take steps to protect the estate and see that Mrs. Amherst's wishes are carried out. I will apply to the court for the following:

1. to have you removed as executor,

2. to request that you receive no executor's fee,

3. to compel the return of the items to the estate, and

4. for an order that you must pay my legal costs.

I look forward to confirmation from you that the items have been returned within the stated time.

Yours truly,

Janet Silver

2
Grounds for Contesting a Will

Non-lawyers tend to call all estate-related lawsuits "contesting the will." However, that is not legally accurate. Contesting a will means bringing a legal challenge to knock down the will in its entirety. The end result of a successful will contest is that there is no longer a valid will in place.

Most lawsuits involving wills and estates are not actually trying to bring the whole will down. In many cases, the goal is to leave the will standing but to change the distribution among certain beneficiaries. In other cases, the goal of the lawsuit is to remove an executor or to pass an executor's accounts or to compel a party related to the estate to carry out certain steps. In other words, the person bringing the lawsuit is not actually attacking the will at all, but is disputing some step or situation that has arisen in the estate administration.

The purpose of this chapter is to help you determine what you should be challenging or contesting based on the facts of your case. You can only work with a legal ground that actually fits your situation. It's important to understand not just how you can attack a will, but also what would happen if you won. If you contest the will and you are successful in having the will declared invalid, then what happens with the estate? Would it be better for you and for other people to bring some other challenge instead? This is a difficult part of litigation to work through on your own, but the information in the next sections should help you clarify how the lawsuits play out.

1. The Three Basic Types of Estate Lawsuits

In this book, we have organized the types of lawsuits involving estates into three basic categories. Your lawsuit will fall into one of these categories:

1. **Contesting the will in a way that, if you are successful, the entire will would be declared invalid.** The

executor appointment would be void so the person named in the will would no longer be the executor. The gifts given to individuals and charitable organizations in the will would no longer be given. Other instructions in the will such as the setting up of trusts would be void.

2. **Claiming against the will for a greater share of the estate based on the fact you're a dependant, while leaving the will and most of its provisions still in place.** If you were successful, the executor appointment would still be valid, as would gifts and trusts. The part that would be different is that someone else — or perhaps, everyone else under the will — is going to receive less because you are receiving more.

3. **All other lawsuits involving wills, including enforcing promises, asking for interpretation of unclear words, and applications such as removal of executors or passing of accounts.** All of these leave the will intact but most make an important change of some kind to it.

It is important to understand what the different phrases and names mean because you will be working in a court environment where all of the judges, lawyers, and clerks will be using those terms. You'll also see those terms in the statutes and cases and on the documents you have to file. You must use the right terminology in order to steer your lawsuit where you want it to go. You must also understand the possible outcomes of the different sorts of estate litigation so that you don't waste time and money working on something that ends up being of no benefit.

In this chapter and in Chapter 4, we will look at the grounds for actually contesting a will with the goal of having a judge declare that the entire will is void. In Chapter 3 we will look at dependants of the deceased claiming for a larger share of the estate. In Chapters 5 through 7 we will look at other kinds of estate-related lawsuits that do not aim to void the entire will. Once you have read all of the chapters relating to types of litigation, you should have a much clearer idea of which of these types fits the facts of your case. Once you know the right name and terminology for your lawsuit, you will find it easy to pinpoint the chapters in this book that will help you get your lawsuit started. You will also find it much easier to speak with judges and court clerks about your case and to do research.

2. On What Grounds Can a Will Be Contested?

As much as some people would love to be able to challenge a will on the basis they simply don't like who is getting what under the will, they are not allowed to do that. There has to be a legal reason, known as the ground, for challenging a will.

Over the hundreds of years that people have been making wills, a body of law has developed to deal with the wills and the challenges to the wills. We now use a combination of statute law, which refers to laws that are created, written down, and passed by the elected government, and case law, which refers to specific cases decided by judges. The statute law lays out the ground rules, such as the fact that a will must be written down and witnessed. The case law interprets and applies the statute law to individual people and situations. Our legal system relies on precedent, which means that when a judge has decided that a legal principle applies, we are bound to follow that lead and resolve cases with similar facts in the same way.

Quite a bit of our wills and estates-related law has been developed through case law and precedent. Though there will be a very thorough discussion of how to find and use precedents later in this book, what you need to know at this early stage is that our law provides only a few grounds on which a will can be contested. Over the years, these grounds have been studied and upheld by the courts and as a result we know a great deal about how to apply them. We also know that your case must fit into one of the grounds in order for you to have the right to contest a will. Those grounds are:

1. Undue influence.

2. Lack of testamentary capacity.

3. Lack of knowledge and approval.

4. Forged or fraudulent will.

5. The will was not properly signed and witnessed.

Though the various grounds are discussed separately in this book, it is certainly possible that more than one of the grounds will fit your scenario. You do not have to choose only one ground to challenge a will; if more than one fits your situation, then you are allowed and, in fact highly encouraged, to use all that fit. You only get one shot at challenging the will so you should not restrict yourself to only one method of challenging if more than one is a good fit.

2.1 Undue influence

This term refers to a situation in which a person makes a will that is not really the will he or she wants to make. He or she makes this will because someone else is pressuring, forcing, threatening, tricking, persuading, or otherwise convincing that person to make that particular will.

Some examples:

- A mother is persuaded by her youngest (adult) daughter to make a will that leaves out all of the other children. The youngest daughter does this by telling her mother repeatedly that the other children don't really care about their mother the way the youngest daughter does.

- A disabled, elderly man is told by his caregiver that unless he makes a will leaving a significant sum to the caregiver, the caregiver is going to put him into a home where he will be alone and mistreated.

- A son takes his elderly mother to a lawyer and directs his mother to make a will leaving her house, which is almost her entire estate, to the son. He rushes her through the process, and answers questions for her when the lawyer asks them. She doesn't want to get her son into trouble and is confused as to what is going on, so she just signs the will.

It is natural that a parent or grandparent is going to be influenced to some degree by the people in his or her life. We all behave in ways that accommodate and please certain people who are important to us, usually without them ever directly asking us for anything. We often want to thank those people for their care and affection over the years. However, all of the examples above show undue influence. This means influence that is over and above the usual and was done on purpose. In other words, someone has gone out of his or her way to apply pressure to an individual to gain some material advantage. Someone has abused his or her position of trust for his or her own gain.

This is by far the most common ground used to contest a will. Most people who want to have a will declared void do so because they believe that their parent or other loved one made a certain gift in his or her will because somebody else made him or her do it.

Some indications that a person might have been unduly influenced:

- The will he or she has now is much different from the one(s) he or she had before.

- The will the person has now goes against plans or ideas the parent or grandparent had repeatedly verbally indicated would happen.

- The will leaves a greater benefit to the person who has been doing the influencing (or the spouse or children of the person doing the influencing) than it does to others.

- There is no logical reason for that person to receive a larger share of the estate.

- The will is in the possession of the person doing the influencing.

- The parent or grandparent whose will it is cannot really explain why he or she has suddenly decided to make a new will.

- The parent or grandparent won't answer questions without checking first with the person who has done the influencing.

- The parent or grandparent is vulnerable or dependent in some way, such as financially, physically, or emotionally, on the person who now stands to gain from the new will.

The elements of undue influence:

1. Someone influenced the testator in some way, such as threats, force, trickery, lies, persuasion, shaming, isolation, control over daily living, or persistent requests. It is likely to be a combination of more than one method.

2. The influence overpowered the testator's mental or emotional freedom so that the testator felt he or she had no choice but to go along with it.

3. The testator made a will that he or she would not have made without that influence.

The usual steps when disputing a will on the ground of undue influence:

1. The executor presents the will to the court and applies for a grant of probate.

2. Someone objects to the will on the grounds of undue influence.

3. The matter is set for a chambers hearing in which the person who has objected to the will has the responsibility of showing that suspicious circumstances existed at the time the will was made. This means the person objecting has to convince the judge that there is an actual issue with the will that deserves to be heard at a trial.

4. To prepare for that application, the parties prepare briefs and sworn affidavits, file them at the court, and give copies to all other parties.

5. The matter is heard in chambers. If the judge agrees there is a triable issue, the matter is scheduled for a full trial. If the judge does not agree, the matter is over. This step is to weed out the applications that are brought frivolously

or by parties who really should not be wasting court time on flimsy cases.

6. The parties gather medical evidence, expert evidence, etc.

2.2 Lack of testamentary capacity

In order for a will to be valid, the person whose will it is must have testamentary capacity. All jurisdictions in Canada have rules about who can make a will, including such things as having reached a certain age. When it comes to contesting wills, though, the part of capacity that becomes important is usually mental capacity.

This means that you can contest a will on the ground that the person who made the will did not have the mental ability to understand what he or she was doing.

Since wills have been around for hundreds of years, so has estate litigation. Over the years, our courts have addressed the issue of testamentary capacity numerous times. This has resulted in a body of law that clarifies what it means for a person to have testamentary capacity. Because of these cases, we can look at any given situation or person and apply a legal test to see whether or not a person had testamentary capacity when making his or her will. The basic elements of that test are:

1. The person who makes and signs a will (known as the testator) must understand that he or she is making a will and must understand the effect of that will. In other words, the testator should understand that he or she is making a plan to give away his or her estate after death.

2. The person must know the nature and value of his or her estate. This doesn't necessarily mean that the person must know to the dollar what he or she owns, but it does mean that the testator should have a pretty good idea. For example, the testator should know that he or she owns a house, or has sold his or her business, or that he or she has substantial cash in the bank.

3. The person must understand the consequences of including and excluding certain people under his or her will. For example, the testator must be able to understand the necessity of supporting dependants. The testator must recall and understand who is in his or her family and have reasons for including or excluding them.

4. The person must be free of any "disorder of the mind" which may influence his or her views. "Disorder of the mind" is a broad, generic description that can apply to anything from mental illness to age-related dementia to the effect of strong medication.

In order to challenge a will on the basis that the testator did not have testamentary capacity, you will have to prove that one or more of these elements was not present. It is also important to note that testamentary capacity must be present at two key times. One is at the time the testator gives the lawyer instructions to prepare the will. The other is at the time the testator signs the will. Usually with homemade wills there is only one relevant time since no instructions are given to a lawyer.

Occasionally a person makes a will that upsets someone or is unpopular with some family members. It is essential to understand that as adults, we are entitled to make unusual or unpopular decisions, even with our wills. Not everyone has to agree with us. However, when the upsetting will is revealed, sometimes unhappy family members who don't like the terms of the will leap to the conclusion that the maker of the will simply did not know what he or she was doing. An astonishing number of families decide that the deceased lacked capacity even when they know nothing at all about testamentary capacity, because it seems like a better explanation to them than accepting that the testator simply didn't want them to inherit anything.

However, challenging a will on the basis of lack of capacity is not easy; you have to get inside the mind of another person at another time and somehow prove what he or she was thinking. If you are considering challenging a will on the basis that the person lacked mental capacity when he or she made the will, first take a long, serious look at the idea. Is it true that the person in question didn't know who was involved or didn't understand what was happening, or did he or she simply make a will that you don't like? Is it your disappointment talking or is there really a legal issue that needs a judge to sort out? If it's the case that you simply don't like it, then you do not have a case. If you don't think it's fair that someone else got more than you did, that does not mean that the testator didn't know what he or she was doing. All it means is that you don't like it. In wills law, you don't have to like it. In Canada, we do not have the legal right to challenge a will based on our disappointment.

2.3 Lack of knowledge and approval

It's the law that a person must have knowledge of, and approve of, the contents of his or her will in order for the will to be valid.

This means people must understand that they are making a will, they must know what it says, and they must approve of what it says. Though in some ways this sounds similar to lack of testamentary capacity, it is not quite the same. When you are alleging lack of

testamentary capacity, your point is that the testator simply could not have understood the will — or any will — because of his or her mental shortcomings. However, when dealing with the ground of lack of knowledge and approval, you are alleging that a testator might have full mental capacity and still not realize what was in the will or what it might mean.

This kind of challenge may be brought if the testator did not know that certain things were in the will. For example, perhaps the family member who helped the testator make a will slipped in a substantial gift to himself or herself without telling the testator. Or perhaps the testator was not aware of what he or she owned because his or her spouse had always handled the family finances, and after the spouse's death one of the kids managed things. Another possibility is that the testator was never able to find out the value of his or her share in the family business.

This kind of claim also applies to situations in which a testator is not aware of the value of his or her estate. Perhaps the testator is not aware that the old farmstead and lands have quadrupled in value over the last ten years, or that the family business in which he or she still holds shares is booming. This makes a difference because a testator who doesn't realize the value of the estate might think he or she is treating the children equally when one gets a bank account with $10,000 and the other gets "everything else." If the testator doesn't realize that "everything else" is worth millions of dollars, then the testator is not really aware of the contents of his or her will.

As you can see, there are various circumstances that could give rise to a person simply not realizing the impact of his or her will even though the person was not mentally incapacitated, as long as there was a logical, provable reason that he or she was not aware of the contents or the meaning of the will.

It is very rare that a case is brought to court only on the ground of lack of knowledge and approval of contents, though it is perfectly legal to do so. Much of the time this ground is combined with undue influence, particularly when it is being alleged that a particular person had controlling influence over the testator. It may also be combined effectively with a claim alleging a lack of testamentary capacity. In terms of strategy, it may be a good idea to combine the two grounds. A judge may be willing to believe that the testator did not fully understand his or her will even if the judge is not willing to find that the testator lacked mental capacity. By combining the two grounds you have built in a back-up ground in case your first point fails.

When a will is signed by an adult in front of two witnesses, there is a presumption of knowledge and approval in that the law presumes that the testator has knowledge and approval of the contents of the will. If the law presumes it, then nobody has to prove it. The exception to that general rule is that a person sending a will to probate does have to prove knowledge and approval if —

1. the testator was blind,

2. the testator was illiterate,

3. the testator did not speak the language of the will, or

4. someone else signed for the testator for any reason.

If any of those situations exists, then there must be affidavit evidence from one of the witnesses explaining how the will was signed and how the testator had knowledge and approval of the contents. The responsibility lies on the person who says the will is valid to show that it is actually valid.

In most cases, the situations listed above do not exist and the issue set before the court has more to do with circumstances such as the will seeming to be uncharacteristic of the testator or beyond his or her understanding. Because the law presumes that the testator understood and approved the will, anyone who wants to challenge that presumption has to show the court that there are suspicious circumstances regarding the will. Here are some questions you might consider when trying to establish that there were suspicious circumstances:

1. Is the will homemade? Did a family member or friend or someone else write the will for the testator? Lack of legal advice can be an extremely important point in this type of case, as you should expect that someone working with a lawyer would have had the will explained to him or her, but otherwise there is no assumption that the testator was fully advised. There likely isn't even any evidence that the will was even read over by the testator first.

2. Are the contents of the will noticeably different from wills that the testator had made in the past? If so, are there logical explanations for such extreme changes?

3. Are the contents of the will consistent with any comments or promises that the testator may have made during his or her lifetime? The most frequent example of this type of comment is a parent's repeated promise that all of the children would be treated equally.

4. Is the language used in the will too complex for the testator to understand?

This could be the case if the testator did not finish a basic education, or if the will is written in a language that is not the testator's first language.

5. Was the testator a hands-on investor or handler of his or her own money? Or had he or she relied on a family member for financial management for some time? This is a tricky one because many seniors ask their adult children to assist with banking while still remaining completely aware of their finances. The problem might arise with someone who either pays little attention to finances or is deliberately excluded from financial decisions by the person helping him or her.

If you are successful in persuading a judge that there are suspicious circumstances surrounding the will, you will have overcome, or rebutted, the presumption that the will is valid. Then you have passed your first hurdle and the focus shifts. It then becomes the responsibility of the person who says the will is valid to prove that it's valid. All of this takes quite a bit of work. The usual steps include:

1. The executor sends the will to the court for probate.

2. You file a caveat to halt the probate process.

3. You file a Statement of Claim and affidavit alleging that there are suspicious circumstances that lead you to believe the testator did not have knowledge and approval of the contents of the will.

4. The executor replies with an affidavit of his or her own.

5. The question of whether there are suspicious circumstances is heard in chambers. If you are successful, then the matter is set down for a trial. If you are not successful, that is the end of the issue.

2.4 Forged or fraudulent will

This ground for challenging a will is the one seen least often in our courts. This is partly because it is particularly tough to prove that a will is forged. Most of the time, the case relies on a handwriting expert who may or may not provide a conclusive report about whether the signature on the will appears to be the same as signatures made by the testator in other circumstances.

Another important source of evidence is that of the witnesses to the will, assuming there were any witnesses. If no witnesses can be found, or their recall of the situation is vague, a person contesting the will would have a better chance of proving a case of forgery simply because there would be nobody who could give contradictory evidence.

It's important to note that when you are alleging that a will is forged or fraudulent, the responsibility for proving the case is on you. It is not up to the executor or anyone else to prove that the will is valid; you are the one with the burden of giving the evidence of what is wrong with the will. It's also important to realize that because this situation involves fraud and forgery — both of which could lead to criminal charges against someone — the judge will hold you to a higher standard than is usual in estate litigation.

These cases tend to be decided on details, some of which can be very subtle. Here are some ideas to consider when wondering whether a will is a forgery or fraud:

1. **Do some of the pages seem to have been replaced?** You might be able to

tell this if the paper is a different colour, size, or texture, or the font used in the text is different from one page to another.

2. **Are there initials at the bottom of some pages but not on others?** Do the initials seem to be the same on all pages? Is the ink the same?

3. **Does the signature appear to be different from what you are used to seeing from the testator on letters, cards, cheques, or other written material?** When you gather several samples of the deceased's handwriting from various sources, does the signature on the will seem the same?

4. **Was the will homemade?** Wills that have been safeguarded in the lawyer's office or a safety deposit box for years are more reliable than those kept at the home of a relative or friend of the testator.

5. **Are there corrections, correction fluid, or erasures in the will?** If the testator made the change himself or herself at the time the will was made, it would have been initialled by the testator and both of the witnesses.

6. **Was there a delay in someone bringing forth the will?** Did quite a bit of time elapse while everyone looked for a will, only to have a family member suddenly find a will that happens to benefit him or her or his or her family?

7. **Are there signs that pages have been removed, such as extra staple holes or tears in the corners of the pages?**

2.5 The will was not properly signed and witnessed

Every province and territory in Canada has rules about how wills are supposed to be signed and witnessed in order for them to be valid. When those rules, which are generally referred to as the signing formalities, are not followed, the will is most likely to be declared invalid. In other cases, as you will see from the subsequent section of this book, the errors in signing and witnessing may be fixed by the court.

In every province, a will must be in writing. At this time, videotaped or oral wills are not legally acceptable in Canada and there is only one published case of a will written on an electronic tablet being accepted as valid. Some provinces in Canada allow holograph wills as valid wills. A holograph will is one that is 100 percent in the handwriting (or footwriting or mouthwriting) of the testator. As mentioned, a will that is a combination of handwriting and typing or a will that contains the handwriting of some other person is not a holograph will. A true holograph will must be signed and dated by the testator but does not need witnesses. Because of the less stringent standards for witnessing holograph wills, it's rare that these wills are challenged on the ground of improper execution. They are, of course, frequently in court for interpretation help and many other reasons, but generally not for lack of proper formalities.

A will must be signed by the testator (the person whose will it is). Legally it is possible for someone to sign on behalf of the testator in unusual circumstances, if that person signs in the presence of the testator and is directed to do so by the testator. Though this is rarely done, it could be the case that a testator was too ill or too badly injured to physically hold a pen to sign. Ideally, this would occur only where there were witnesses available to swear to the fact that the person signing was actually directed by the testator to sign for him or her. Without such witnesses, the will is extremely vulnerable to being declared invalid.

Most wills are known as formal wills. This simply means that they are not in the handwriting of the testator. Usually they are produced on a computer, printed, and signed. In other cases, the will could be the product of a template-type "will kit" which combines typewritten and handwritten portions of the will, or a will handwritten by someone other than the testator. All of these wills are considered formal wills and as such there are strict rules about witnessing in order for them to be valid wills.

The rule for signing and witnessing is the same across the country though it is worded somewhat differently from place to place. The testator must sign the will in the presence of two witnesses, both of whom must be present at the same time. Then each witness must sign the will in the presence of the testator and in the presence of the other witness. In other words, everyone must sign in front of everyone else before anyone is allowed to leave the room.

There are restrictions on who can be the witness to a will. These are the same all across the country. The witness may not be a beneficiary of the will or the spouse/common law partner of a beneficiary of the will. If the will is otherwise valid, having the wrong person witness the will does not destroy the entire will. It does, however, invalidate the part of the will that leaves a gift to the witness.

When a will is produced that has the signatures of the testator and the witnesses, the law presumes that the will was properly executed. If you want to challenge a will based on improper signing and witnessing, it is your responsibility to produce facts that cast doubt on the signing and witnessing. Unless you do that, there is no responsibility on the executor or anyone else to prove the will was properly executed.

3. Curative Provisions in Legislation

Some provinces have laws that allow a judge to fix a will that has defects in the signing or witnessing that might otherwise cause a will to be invalid. As described above, all wills must comply with the formal requirements set down in the provincial wills law. A will that has an error or missing words is considered to be *noncompliant* with the legislation and normally could not be accepted by the probate court as a valid will. However, when a province has these laws that allow the will to be fixed — known as *curative provisions* — you can send a will to probate on the basis that the will is *substantially compliant* with the law. In other words, you can say that the will should still be admitted as valid even though something is missing.

Your point would be that the will is substantially or mostly compliant except for one element. You would be claiming that the missing date or the signature in the wrong place or the mixed-up numbering of paragraphs was simply a logistical error that should not impact a will that otherwise contains the wishes and instructions of the deceased. The idea behind it is to do everything possible to give effect to the deceased's wishes.

As with any court application, you cannot get what you want just by asking for it. Wills can be held to be valid even though they don't strictly comply with the law if there is clear evidence that the testator meant the

CHECKLIST 1
IS THE WILL PROPERLY EXECUTED?

1. [   ]   Did the testator sign the will at the end of the document?

2. [   ]   Did the testator sign it in front of two witnesses?

3. [   ]   Were the two witnesses in the room the whole time that the testator was reading and signing?

4. [   ]   Did both of the witnesses sign the will at the end of the document?

5. [   ]   Did both of the witnesses sign in front of the testator and in front of each other?

6. [   ]   Is the will dated?

7. [   ]   If anything was crossed out or handwritten in the will, did the testator and both the witnesses (the same two that signed) initial the changes?

8. [   ]   Are either of the witnesses beneficiaries of the will?

9. [   ]   Are either of the witnesses spouses of beneficiaries in the will?

In order for the will to be valid, all of these questions must be answered with a yes, except for questions 8 and 9, which must be answered with a no.

---

document to be his or her will and that the document contains the testator's intentions. Whether you are attacking the will or defending it, you must consider what evidence exists of what the testator intended.

The nature of the mistake is important too; was it simply a typo made by a receptionist that nobody noticed at the time? Was the wrong name put into the document? Was a line or word left out? Some mistakes are considered worse than others. In Canada, the courts have fixed mistakes such as those mentioned in this paragraph, but so far they have refused to declare unsigned wills as being valid.

The purpose of the curative legislation is to ensure that a will does not fail and all of a testator's plans collapse because of a technical mistake. Before beginning a lawsuit on the basis that a will was not properly executed, make sure you know whether your province has this type of law. Otherwise you might launch your lawsuit against a will just to find that the court has the power to fix it and you will have wasted your time and money. Table 1 shows which provinces and territories have the kind of curative law that allows judges to fix mistakes in wills.

TABLE 1
CURATIVE PROVISIONS BY PROVINCE

Province or Territory	Curative Provisions?	Where to Find Them
Alberta	yes	section 37, *Wills and Succession Act*
British Columbia	yes	section 58, *Wills, Estates and Succession Act*
Manitoba	yes	Section 23, *Wills Act*
New Brunswick	yes	section 35.1, *Wills Act*
Newfoundland and Labrador	no	N/A
Northwest Territories	no	N/A
Nova Scotia	yes	Section 8A, *Wills Act*
Nunavut	yes	Section 13.1, *Wills Act*
Ontario	no	N/A
Prince Edward Island	yes	section 70, *Probate Act*
Saskatchewan	yes	section 37, *Wills Act*
Yukon	no	N/A

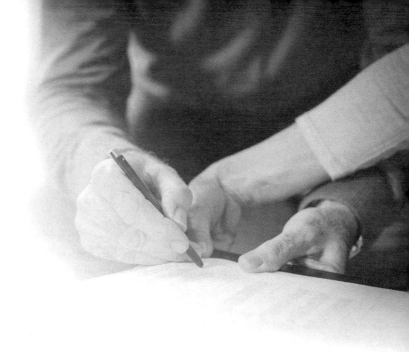

3
Relief Claims

Much of the litigation involving estates is clustered around a concept called dependant's relief. This concept is, simply, that a person who was financially dependent upon the deceased is entitled to receive support from the deceased's estate. If the dependant believes that he or she was not given adequate support in the deceased's will, the dependant may sue the estate to ask for a greater share of the estate assets than the will provided. This is a type of claim that does not invalidate the entire will.

The same kind of lawsuit is available to dependants if the deceased died without a will and the estate is being distributed according to the laws of intestacy. When a person dies without a valid will, the laws of intestacy set out the portions that the family members will get from the deceased's estate. The dependant who believes that he or she has been short-changed can still go through the court and ask that he or she get a larger share of the estate.

This kind of lawsuit is not really a contest of the will because regardless of whether the claim is successful or not, the will itself will still stand as valid. The executor will still be the executor. Provisions regarding funeral arrangements, executor's fees, the age of inheritance, trusts, and many other matters will still stand undisturbed. The gifts to the beneficiaries may be varied by the court but the general structure of the will is going to be the same. All you are asking is that a share that is directed by the will to go to someone else should be reduced so that you can have a larger portion.

1. Who Is Entitled to Ask for Dependant's Relief?

There are certain people in most people's lives who are, by law, legal dependants. They are the people who automatically have the right to financial support from your estate, and by extension, have the right to ask the court for dependant's relief. These dependants are defined in the legislation of each province and territory but all parts of Canada include the following people as dependants:

1. **Your spouse.** In every province and territory this includes a married spouse. It does not include a common law spouse everywhere, though. Check Table 2 to see whether your province includes common law spouses as dependants.

2. **Your minor children.**

3. **Your adult children who have a disability that will likely prevent them from earning a living to support themselves.** This is generally thought to include a severe physical or mental disability such as Down's syndrome or a debilitating injury brought about by a motor vehicle accident.

In Alberta, the legislation also specifically includes your children up to age 22 who are attending a postsecondary educational institution.

Always remember that when you qualify as a dependant under the law, you are entitled to ask the court to change the estate distribution so that you get more. You are not necessarily going to win. You are not automatically entitled to get more from the estate. Your right is to ask, not necessarily to receive. Not every case succeeds. Even if the matter goes all the way to trial, the judge may not agree that you should get more of the estate.

Not every dependant is able to conduct a lawsuit because of the condition that creates the dependency in the first place. An adult child with a mental disability may simply not be able to understand the consequences of the will or to instruct a lawyer. A dependant in this situation is not necessarily left out in the cold, however; a person using an Enduring Power of Attorney (Representation Agreement in BC) or a court-appointed guardianship or trusteeship is entitled to sue the estate on behalf of the disabled dependant. If the disabled person in question doesn't have a legal representative in place, the court might appoint someone to represent that person's interests. That representative would be called a guardian or trustee *ad litem* and would only have legal authority while the lawsuit was going on.

One of the grey areas for this type of lawsuit involves an adult child of the person who passed away who was financially dependent on the parent even though the child had never had any diagnosis of a disability. Sometimes the individuals who begin lawsuits for dependant's relief do so simply because they've always lived with the parent, have never held a job that provided much to live on, and simply cannot imagine now being out on their own. There may not be an actual disability other than reluctance to support oneself. The fact that the parent allowed or perhaps even encouraged that scenario lets the adult child believe that he or she is entitled to have it continue.

In other cases, there are adult children who genuinely were dependent on their parents because of an undiagnosed mental illness, an addiction, economic misfortune, attendance at postsecondary education, or many other reasons.

I refer to these cases as grey areas because they do not fit the traditional model of a disability that would prevent someone from earning a living. Theoretically there is no reason why any particular adult person could not earn a living like anyone else. In other cases the individual might fit the description perfectly but there has never been any medical documentation to prove the disability. Perhaps

TABLE 2
WHO HAS THE RIGHT TO CLAIM DEPENDANT'S RELIEF?

Province or Territory	Married Spouse	Common Law Spouse	Minor Child	Adult Child with a Disability	Anyone Else?
Alberta	Yes	Yes, if spouse qualifies as an Adult Interdependent Partner	Yes	Yes	• Children up to age 22 who are in school
British Columbia	Yes	Yes, if lived together for 2 years	Yes	Yes	No
Manitoba	Yes	Yes, if lived together for 3 years	Yes	Yes	• Former common law partner if separated less than 3 years before death of the deceased • Divorced spouse if there is a support order in place • Parent, grandparent, grandchild, or sibling of the deceased who was financially dependent upon the deceased
New Brunswick	Yes	Yes, if cohabiting within the year before the deceased died	Yes	Yes	• Any person who the deceased is obligated to support • The judge may refuse to make an order in favour of any person if his or her character or conduct is such as, in the opinion of the judge, to disentitle that person
Newfoundland and Labrador	Yes	No	Yes	Yes	No
Northwest Territories	Yes	Yes (no time limit imposed by law)	Yes	Yes	• Stepchild • A person who at the time of the death of the deceased was acting as a foster parent of the children of the deceased in the same household and who was dependent on the deceased for support
Nova Scotia	Yes	No	Yes	Yes	No

TABLE 2 — CONTINUED

Nunavut	Yes	Yes, if lived together for 2 years or have a child together	Yes	Yes	• A person who at the time of the death of the deceased was acting as a foster parent of the children of the deceased in the same household and who was dependent on the deceased for support
Ontario	Yes	Yes, if lived together for 3 years or have a child together	Yes	Yes	• A parent or sibling of the deceased to whom the deceased was providing support • A divorced spouse if there is a support order in place
Prince Edward Island	Yes	Yes, if lived together for 3 years	Yes	Yes	• A parent, grandparent, or descendant of the deceased who had been financially dependent on the deceased for at least 3 years • A divorced spouse who had been dependent on the deceased for financial support for at least 3 years
Saskatchewan	Yes	Yes, if lived together for 2 years or have a child together	Yes	Yes	No
Yukon	Yes	Yes, if lived together for 1 year	Yes	Yes (defined as age 16 or older)	• A parent, grandparent, or descendant of the deceased who had been financially dependent on the deceased for at least 3 years • A divorced spouse who had been dependent on the deceased for financial support for at least 3 years

up until the death of the testator, the medical situation was handled within the family without the need for medical documents. In other words, the situation doesn't fit nicely into the framework contemplated by the law. This doesn't mean that a "grey area" case cannot succeed, but winning is an uphill battle.

2. What Exactly Are You Suing For?

This type of lawsuit relies on the phrase "adequate support," which is open to interpretation. In most parts of Canada, this is all the law says about how much you can have from the estate. It does not give a percentage or even a formula for determining an amount. The math behind the lawsuit is left open this way to allow for the wide variety of cases that come before the courts, but it is not particularly helpful if you are hoping for an equation or percentage to tell you how much to claim. Once you have established that you are a dependant, you then have to prove that whatever you were left under the will (or intestacy law) does not provide you with adequate support.

Everyone's idea of what is adequate for their lifestyle is different. Those who are used to an annual income in the hundreds of thousands of dollars have a significantly higher comfort threshold than people who are used to a more mainstream income. It will be up to you to determine what dollar amount you wish to request. Remember that it will also be up to you to show why you need that amount.

This application involves you providing the court with a lot of personal and financial information. In order to show that you need money from the estate, you will have to show what your current expenses are and what you currently bring in from other sources. This may feel invasive but if you are claiming that you don't have enough money, you are going to have to reveal what you do have. There is no way around that.

Remember though that this kind of application is not just about covering the basic bills. It's about maintaining a lifestyle comparable to the one you would have enjoyed had your spouse (or other supporter) not passed away. If, for example, you were married to the deceased person and together you two led a comfortable lifestyle, you have every right to expect that lifestyle to continue if the funds exist. You are not expected to suddenly live in poverty upon the death of your spouse while his or her other family members gain a windfall. Assuming there are actually enough assets in the estate to fund a lifestyle similar to what you maintained before your spouse's death, you may object to those assets going to someone else while you must now live a bare-bones existence. This is especially true if the two of you spent years building up assets together in order to enjoy a comfortable retirement.

3. Ramifications for Individuals Receiving Disability Support from the Government

Though it's not unusual to see that a person with a disability has managed to obtain employment, most of the individuals claiming dependant's relief do so because of a severe disability. In general this means that the person in question cannot work and therefore relies on federal and provincial government subsidies to survive. In law, an adult child who relies on public assistance is considered more in need of parental support than other adult children who are able to earn their own living. It is also considered socially right (meaning, the courts will generally favour) that a parent support his or her own children if possible, rather than have the public support that child. This structure of goals and values is reflected in our legal system. Most adult children with severe disabilities who are not provided adequate support under a parent's will are likely to be successful in their applications for a greater share of the parent's estate.

This may present a dilemma for a disabled adult child who is considering making the claim for dependant's relief. On one hand, the security of having a nest egg to provide financial security for the future would bring peace of mind and perhaps improve current living conditions. On the other hand, owning that nest egg will probably cause the disabled child to forfeit government social assistance benefits that he or she currently receives. If the nest egg happens to be in the hundreds of thousands of dollars, perhaps the loss of government benefits is not a concern. However, most people don't inherit hundreds of thousands of dollars and the potential loss of government benefits might have a serious, negative impact. In some provinces, the government benefit plans provide a basic monthly allowance. In almost all provinces such plans also provide very valuable assistance with medical, optical, dental, housing, homecare, and transportation expenses.

If you inherit more than the amount allowed by your provincial plan, you may be cut off from your benefits entirely.

Note that this discussion is about the social assistance or disability type of benefit. Individuals who receive support from private pensions, Canada Pension Plan, Workers' Compensation, Veterans' Affairs, Registered Disability Savings Plans (RDSP), Old Age Security, Employment Insurance, investments, Henson Trusts, disability insurance policies, or other sources are not affected by inheriting money. In addition, if the amounts from those other sources are large enough, the recipient may not feel the loss of the provincial social assistance benefits. Every case is unique. As you consider challenging the will, make sure you understand whether winning a sum of money would impact other financial support. If it does have an impact, make sure you understand any risk to your financial well-being. See Table 3.

4. What Factors Affect the Outcome of a Dependant's Relief Application?

As mentioned earlier, not every lawsuit of this type will succeed. The judge hears each one on its own merits. Even assuming that you have proven that what you are given in the will is inadequate for your support, you might not get what you want from the estate. This is because no claim against an estate exists in a vacuum; there are always other people involved whose positions might have an impact on your lawsuit. Below you will see a discussion of some of the major factors that a judge will consider when he or she is hearing this type of claim and considering what you might get as your award.

4.1 Competing claims

You may not be the only person who is entitled to support from the estate. You may be a spouse who believes he or she needs more support, but there may also be minor children or a disabled adult child in the picture. Any other dependants of the deceased are considered competing claims because they too have rights. The judge is not going to ignore other claimants' situations in favour of just one. Everyone has to be taken into consideration.

This does not mean that a spouse's claim cannot succeed if there are minor children, or that a minor child's claim cannot succeed if there is a disabled adult. It only means that the judge will consider everyone when making up his or her mind about what is fair. The more

TABLE 3
ASSETS THAT MAY OR MAY NOT INTERFERE WITH RECEIPT OF GOVERNMENT BENEFITS

Province or Territory	Benefit Program	Assets You Can Own without Interfering with Benefits	Assets That Will or Could Interfere with Benefits
Alberta	Assured Income for the Severely Handicapped (AISH)	<ul><li>Cash and assets of up to $100,000 owned by you and your cohabiting partner</li><li>Income tax refunds</li><li>RDSP</li><li>LIRA</li><li>A home that you live in or one quarter-section of farmland that includes the home</li><li>If you live in an institution, the residence may be occupied by your cohabiting partner or your dependent child</li><li>Household goods and furniture</li><li>A vehicle</li><li>A second vehicle adapted for a disability</li><li>Prepaid funeral</li><li>Insurance funds that are used to replace items</li><li>Funds received from Alberta Child Welfare class action settlement</li><li>Alberta Family Employment Tax Credit</li><li>Canada Child Tax Benefit</li><li>Structured settlement due to a personal injury claim</li><li>Award or prize given in recognition of outstanding academic or community achievement</li><li>Cash and non-cash gifts from First Nations band</li><li>Childrens' services payments under *Child, Youth and Family Enhancement Act*</li><li>CPP death benefit</li><li>Payments under *Victims of Crime Act*</li><li>Any income earned by a dependent child who is in school full time</li></ul>	<ul><li>Earned income of more than $800 per month for an individual or $1,950 for a family</li><li>Pension income</li><li>Cash and assets of any kind – real or personal – worth more than $100,000</li><li>Shares of an incorporated business</li><li>Spousal support</li><li>CPP Disability, Retirement, or Survivor's Benefit</li><li>Employment income of a Treaty Indian earned on reserve</li><li>Employment insurance (EI) and maternity benefits</li><li>Trust income deemed payable to the beneficiary of a trust if you or your cohabiting partner are the beneficiary</li><li>Veterans' Affairs benefits</li><li>Workers' Compensation wage replacement benefits</li></ul>

TABLE 3 — CONTINUED

		• Payments under Federal Extraordinary Assistance Plan (Federal HIV Settlement) • Payments made directly to a vendor or service provider on your behalf • Education or training grant, artist's grant, or a grant to start a business • GST rebate • Home renovation grant • OAS Guaranteed Income Supplement • Income tax refunds • Inheritance as long as it falls within the asset limit • Life insurance proceeds • Land claim settlements • Alberta resource rebate • Student loan • Lottery winnings as long as they fall within the asset limit	
British Columbia	Income Assistance for the Disabled	• $5,000 cash (increased to $10,000 for a family with dependants) • Employment earnings of $800 per month • A home of any value that you live in • Family Bonus income • GST credit and Child Tax Credit • One vehicle of any value • Household goods, furniture • Tools of your trade • Funds held in a Henson Trust, though there are restrictions on how it can be spent • RDSP • Crisis Supplement	• A nondiscretionary trust that holds more than $200,000 (this is the kind you can set up yourself with the help of a lawyer) • Earned income of more than $800 per month • Inheritance
Manitoba	Employment and Income Assistance (EIA)	• Liquid assets up to $4,000 per person to a maximum of $16,000 per household • Earnings up to $200 per month • A residence you live in and the land the house stands on • Household items and furniture	• Inheritance over the asset limit • Earnings of more than $200 per month • Employment earnings of a spouse or cohabiting partner • Any real estate held in a trust • Income or growth on assets

TABLE 3 — CONTINUED

		<ul><li>Inventory and equipment essential to carrying on a viable farming or business operation</li><li>Funds held in a Henson Trust up to $200,000, with restrictions on what can be purchased</li><li>RDSP up to $200,000 (note that the combined value of trusts and RDSPs cannot exceed $200,000)</li><li>RESP</li><li>Gifts of a nonrecurring nature up to $100 each</li><li>Payments under Federal Extraordinary Assistance Plan (Federal HIV Settlement)</li><li>Payments under federal Hepatitis C settlement</li><li>Compensation related to a claim of abuse at a residential school</li><li>Canada Student Grant for students with disabilities</li><li>Land claims settlements</li><li>Canada Child Benefit</li><li>Payments received for support of a foster child</li><li>GST rebate</li><li>Start-up and operating grants for daycares under the Manitoba *Child Day Care Act*</li><li>70% of gross earnings from boarders</li><li>Payments under Energy Costs Assistance Program</li></ul>	<ul><li>Trust or RDSP funds if the combined value of all trusts and RDSP together exceed $200,000</li><li>A second residence</li><li>A vehicle</li></ul>
New Brunswick	Extended Benefits Program	<ul><li>$10,000 in liquid assets</li><li>$50,000 in an RRSP</li><li>Earned income of $500 per month plus 30% of earned income above $500</li><li>Cash surrender value of a lie insurance policy</li><li>A home that you live in plus the land on which the home stands</li><li>One vehicle</li><li>Tools of your trade</li><li>Funds held in a Henson Trust</li></ul>	<ul><li>Assets that are liquid or easily converted to liquid, i.e., cash, bank account, Canada Savings Bonds, investments, of more than $10,000 (not including your RRSP)</li><li>Income from RDSP and/or trust fund of more than $800 per month</li><li>Inheritance</li></ul>

TABLE 3 — CONTINUED

		• A nondiscretionary trust fund up to $200,000 • RDSP • Prepaid funeral	
Newfoundland and Labrador	Income Support program	• Cash up to $3,000 for one person or $5,500 for a couple • Funds held in a Henson Trust • Funds held in a Support Trust to a maximum of $100,000, as long as the 2% a year rule is followed • RDSP up to a maximum of $200,000 • RESP • Payments under Federal Extraordinary Assistance Plan (Federal HIV Settlement) • Income tax refunds for 2010 or later • Child welfare allowances • Payments under a Youth Services Agreement • Earnings of dependants • Payments received from the Newfoundland and Labrador Housing Corporation Educational Incentive Allowance • Land claims settlements • Payment received from the Hebron Community Commemorative Fund • Universal Child Care benefits • Student loans (if you have dependants) • A Common Experience Payment made by the Government of Canada to former students of Indian Residential Schools • A General Compensation Payment or Abuse Compensation Payment made by the Government of Canada • Prepaid funeral • Severance package • RRSP of no more than $10,000 for a period of 90 days	• Payments under the Canada Pension Plan, Old Age Security benefits, or Veterans' Allowance • Compensation under the *Workplace Health, Safety and Compensation Act* • Employment Insurance (EI) benefits • Federal training allowance • Income resulting from the sale of property or the sale of a fishing licence • Inheritance • Insurance payments • Assets that are liquid or easily converted to liquid, i.e., cash, bank account, Canada Savings Bonds, investments, if more than $3,000

TABLE 3 — CONTINUED

Northwest Territories	Income Assistance Program	• Total assets up to $50,000 • Cash of $300 plus $100 for each dependant • $500 a year income or goods from Treaty No. 8 or No. 11 • $500 a year income or goods from land claims settlement • Funds held in a Henson Trust, with strict limitations on income paid • RDSP • RESP • A home that you live in (of reasonable value) • Household goods and furniture • Tools of your trade or business • One vehicle adapted for disability • Vehicle and equipment for hunting, fishing, and trapping • Worker's Compensation Benefits that replace income • Federal and NWT Child Benefit • CPP Survivor's Benefit paid to a child • Payments made by the Director of Child and Family Services for a foster child • Money paid or payable under a Common Experience Payment, any residential school settlement, or the Hepatitis C settlement	• Income from boarders • Benefits received from charitable organizations • Income from hunting, trapping, and fishing • GST tax credit • Gifts of cash or items that can be converted to cash • Tax refunds • Training and education grants • Bingo and lottery winnings • Inheritance • Any financial instrument or asset that can be converted to cash within 90 days including real estate, debts owed to you, accounts receivable, investments, bank accounts, life insurance policies, and agreements for sale
Nova Scotia	Employment Support and Income Assistance	• Cash and assets of $2,000 for a single person or $4,000 for a family • A home that you live in • Funds held in a Henson Trust • RDSP • GST rebate • National Child Benefit or Child Disability Benefit • Income your dependent children make while going to school full time • Income tax refunds	• Child maintenance from a former spouse or partner • Employment benefits (EI) • Income from boarders • A nondiscretionary trust of any size • Trust money used for collateral for a loan • Inheritance
Nunavut	Nunavut Disability Support Program	• Cash assets up to $5,000 • A residence you live in (only if reasonable in value)	• Any asset of value that could be converted to cash but has not been converted within 90 days

TABLE 3 — CONTINUED

		• Real property necessary for the operation of a business • Child Tax Benefits • Casual gifts of small value • Payments received for the care of a foster child • The value of essential equipment to carry on hunting, trapping, logging, fishing, or business operations • The value of any money or goods received in accordance with the provisions of Treaty No. 8 or No. 11 • Payments from land claims settlements • Money held in trust for a child that is not available for distribution • Up to $200 per month from a training program • Day-care subsidy • Annual distribution from a co-op • Common Experience payment • Working Income Tax Benefit • RDSP	• Salary or wages • Income from hunting, trapping, logging, fishing, and business • 40% of the gross income received from roomers or lodgers • Benefits from charitable organizations • Spousal and child support • Funds received from a divorce settlement or order • Inheritance • Gifts received regularly or that exceed $40 per month • Bingo and lottery winnings if more than $40 per month • CPP benefits • Income in kind
Ontario	Ontario Disability Support Program (ODSP)	• Cash up to $40,000 for an individual or $50,000 for a couple • A home that you live in • A personal use vehicle • A second vehicle valued up to $15,000 if it is necessary to maintain employment • Tools of your trade • Business assets up to $20,000 that are necessary to carry on the business and earn income • RDSP • RESP • Furniture, clothing, household items • Prepaid funeral • Funds received as a court award for pain, suffering, or grief due to the death of someone in the family	• RRSP • TFSA • A house other than the one you live in, unless that house is necessary for the health or well-being of someone in your family • Investments if they exceed your cash limit • Valuable collections or items • Inheritance if it exceeds your cash limit

TABLE 3 — CONTINUED

		<ul><li>Payment received under the Extraordinary Assistance Plan</li><li>Funds held in a Henson Trust</li><li>Cash surrender value of a life insurance policy</li><li>Payment under the Hepatitis C Agreement</li><li>Payment received from the Government of Alberta as compensation for sterilization</li><li>Payment received from class action settlements (too numerous to list here)</li><li>Training allowance while attending the training program full time</li><li>Compensation, other than compensation for loss of income, related to a claim of abuse sustained at an Indian residential school</li><li>Payments made under the Quest for Gold – Ontario Athlete Assistance Program</li><li>Payment made under the Ontario Renovates program</li></ul>	
Prince Edward Island	Disability Support Program (Social Assistance)	<ul><li>Liquid assets up to $900 for a single person or $1,800 for a couple when both receiving disability benefits</li><li>Earned income of $125 plus 10% of the balance of net income</li><li>A home that you live in</li><li>Household items, clothing, furniture</li><li>One vehicle</li><li>Real property that is required as a base for your business, farming, or fishing operation and the items needed to continue that usage (only if the business is viable)</li><li>Woodland that is sufficient to meet your home heating needs</li><li>A farm property that is reasonable to expect will sustain your son or daughter in the future</li><li>Funds held in a Henson Trust</li></ul>	<ul><li>Any assets, liquid, real, or personal that can be converted to cash within 90 days</li><li>Earned income, including wages, tips, commissions, and training allowance</li><li>Self-employed income including farmers, fishermen, babysitters, and tradespersons</li><li>Voluntary deductions from earned income (e.g., Canada Savings Bond, profit-sharing plans, or accessible savings plans)</li><li>Money donated by a charity for a specific purpose (illness, injury) that are over and above what is needed to deal with the purpose</li><li>Funds received as a result of court-ordered actions such as child maintenance or garnishees</li><li>Lottery winnings</li></ul>

TABLE 3 — CONTINUED

		• RDSP • RESP • Insurance proceeds that are used to replace items • Donations from a charity if they are for the purpose of alleviating distress arising from disaster or misfortune • Money from a Canada Student Loan that is used to cover books, tuition, and transportation • Funds received for supporting a foster child • Court or settlement awards for pain, suffering, or grief • GST rebates • Cash received upon divorce or separation on the sale of the family home as long as a new home is purchased within 90 days	• Inheritance • Cash gifts • Insurance settlements • Income tax refunds that exceed the liquid asset limit
Saskatchewan	Saskatchewan Assistance Plan (SAP)	• Cash up to $1,500 for the first family member, $1,500 for the second family member, and $500 for each subsequent family member • A home that you live in • Real and personal property essential to farm or business, including up to a quarter section for the family residence • Funds held in a Henson Trust • RDSP • RESP • Any funds earned by a child attending school full-time • Any amount received for care of a relative under *The Personal Care Homes Act* to a predetermined maximum • 25% of revenue from providing room and board to a non-relative • Insurance proceeds to replace items • Cash surrender value of a life insurance policy • Prepaid funeral up to $7,500	• A house other than the one you live in • Farmland over and above what is essential for farming • Any financial instrument or asset that can be converted to cash within 90 days, including bank accounts, investments, court award of damages, or settlement of a claim • Any proceeds of the sale of your principal residence not used within 4 months to buy a new principal residence • Inheritance

TABLE 3 — CONTINUED

Yukon	Social Assistance and Yukon Supplementary Allowance	• Cash up to $500 for one person or $1,000 for a household of 2 persons, plus $300 for each additional household member • Liquid assets in a form other than cash in the amount of $1,500 for one person or $2,500 for two or more • A residence that you live in • Real property essential for earning income • Tools of your trade up to $5,000 • Funds held in a Henson Trust • RDSP • RESP • Canada Child Benefit • GST rebates • Insurance proceeds that are used to replace items • Income tax refund up to $400 • Prepaid funeral	• Salary, wages, and tips • Rental income from part of your home • Income from trapping, logging, fishing, farming, or business • Employment Insurance (EI) benefits • Child support payments • Grants, bursaries, or scholarships • Inuvialuit Regional Corporation Distribution Payment • Dividends or entitlements from a First Nation • Gifts of more than $125 in a month • Lottery winnings if they exceed the cash limit

Please note that the lists here should give you a good idea of what is allowed under any provincial or territorial plan, but they are not exhaustive. Each plan has its own details, and those details change frequently. Make sure you confirm all details with the plan itself before relying on this chart.

claims that compete with yours, the lower your chances of getting exactly what you want.

In addition to the claims of other dependants, the judge will think about other wishes expressed by the deceased in the will such as gifts to charities and to other beneficiaries. There could also be substantial claims from creditors. All of these other parties wanting a part of the estate may have an impact on your claim.

4.2 Size of the estate

When the deceased was wealthy and his or her estate very large, there is probably enough for everyone to share and be satisfied. However, not all estates contain enough assets to satisfy all of the claims against it. In fact, most do not. In such cases, the judge only has a certain amount of money to work with.

A claim for dependant's relief, like any other claim against an estate, can only be made against the assets that are actually in the estate. It may not be clear at the outset of a lawsuit which assets are actually in an estate. Even though a person may appear to be wealthy, there may be next to nothing in that person's estate depending on how the ownership of assets is set up. The following is an example of that situation.

Lindsay's father passed away, leaving her $10,000 in his will. Lindsay has Multiple Sclerosis and knows that soon she will no longer be able to hold onto her part-time job. She will receive a disability benefit but could really use some extra funds. She worries about the future now that her Dad is no longer around to slip her a few dollars on her birthday or help her when she is really running low. Lindsay is disappointed in the amount her father left to her because he lived in a very large, lovely house with Lindsay's stepmother. He had a lakeside cabin that Lindsay knows is in a very desirable location. He had a pension from putting in many years of work before retirement and is pretty sure he had life insurance as well. It seems that the small amount he left to her is a drop in the bucket. Lindsay launched a claim for dependant's relief against her father's estate. Ultimately, though she qualified as a dependant, there was nothing that could be given to her. Her father's house, cabin, and bank accounts were all held jointly with his wife and so went to his wife automatically. His pension and his life insurance named his wife as his beneficiary so they went to her automatically as well. There was simply nothing in the estate to be shared with Lindsay.

4.3 Other assets you received from the deceased on his or her death

In Lindsay's example in section 4.2, the dependent adult child was left out in the cold because all of the deceased's assets were either jointly owned with another person or were directed to another person by way of beneficiary designation. Let's change that example slightly so that the deceased father had half a million dollars in a bank account in his own name. Let's also say that the claimant was not the daughter, but the wife. Perhaps Lindsay's stepmother believed that she needed that bank account to maintain her lifestyle and therefore made a claim to receive that account based on her status as a dependant.

On the face of the will, neither the daughter nor the wife received much under the estate. This is because the assets mentioned in the example are not in the estate and don't show on the estate inventory. The court will not know about them unless someone provides that information. There would only be a bank account in dispute. If the wife is claiming the bank account and so is the daughter, suddenly those other assets become important and need to be brought to the judge's attention. The judge would need to know that the wife received all of those assets outside of the will. In a balancing act between the wife and the daughter, the fact that the wife had already received a hefty financial amount would make a difference.

4.4 Length of the marriage

If your claim for dependant's relief is based on the fact of marriage (or, in provinces where it is allowed to claim a common law relationship), then the length of the relationship is most likely going to be a factor in whether or not your claim succeeds. If you have supported, helped, or contributed towards the finances or lifestyle of the deceased for 30 years, that is quite a different picture from one in which you did the same for only six months. Your contribution to the relationship is not necessarily directly financial in the sense of you bringing in money to the household. If you and your partner agreed that you would raise the children and run the household rather than work for pay outside the home, your contribution still counts. Your contribution of time, energy, and focus allowed your partner to get on with his or her career and therefore a longer relationship may contribute to receiving a larger award from the court.

4

Resulting Trust and Unjust Enrichment

As mentioned earlier, not all lawsuits involving wills intend to collapse the will in its entirety. The type of lawsuit known as "dependant's relief" was discussed in Chapter 3. Now, we are going to look at some court applications that are seen frequently and are neither trying to crash a will nor trying to obtain a greater share of the estate for a dependent.

It is impossible to list here every possible reason for litigation; there are too many variations on the facts and the issues. You will find though, despite the infinite variety of factors, certain themes and laws are constant throughout. In this chapter we will look at some applications that are frequently brought to court. The vast majority of cases will be covered by these discussions.

1. Resulting Trust and Unjust Enrichment

We have all heard of cases in which a person, now deceased, made a promise to a family member or friend that one day the deceased would leave something to that family member or friend. If the deceased failed to keep the promise, the family member or friend may be left wondering whether he or she has any right to challenge the will to get the item that was promised.

Most of the time, a verbal promise to leave something to someone holds no weight at all and would never succeed as the basis for a lawsuit. But the law says that if certain conditions are met, the family member or friend who was promised something can receive it even though the promise was broken. Those conditions are not met nearly often enough to make some disappointed beneficiaries happy. The good news is that the conditions that have to be met have been very clearly defined by the courts so that these days we have a pretty good idea of whether a case is likely to be successful. Before you decide to proceed on this kind of case, make sure you can meet the conditions.

When you ask the court to enforce the promise made to you, you are asking that the item in question be held in a resulting trust. This simply means that you want the judge to order that the promise made to you results in the estate holding onto the asset in trust for you until it can be transferred or paid to you, as opposed to the estate holding it for the beneficiaries named in the will. Once the judge has made the decision in your favour, the asset in question can be transferred to you or other compensation arranged, as discussed later in this chapter. If you are not successful in establishing that you meet the conditions for a resulting trust, the estate will dispose of the asset according to the will as if you had never made the claim.

Usually with this type of lawsuit, the asset that was promised is real estate. It can be any asset, of course, but generally speaking real estate of some kind is involved. Here is an example:

Jonas' grandfather, Karl, was a cattle rancher. Karl's children were not interested in ranching themselves, and as they grew up they left the ranch to pursue other career paths. From a young age, Jonas showed an interest in the ranch and spent his summer breaks from school working with Karl. They would often talk about the future of the ranch, and from time to time Karl would say, "You know, Jonas, you are the only one in the family who will know how to run this place. One day, when I'm gone, this ranch will be yours. My kids don't want It, but I want it to stay in the family. You're a hard worker and I know you can do it." Knowing that one day he'd own the ranch, Jonas devoted even more time to it. He poured his own money and energy into the upkeep of the buildings and

---

buying more breeding stock. His father offered to pay for Jonas to attend university, but Jonas didn't want to leave the ranch for four years and so he turned down his father's offer. When Karl died several years later, Jonas was shocked and deeply disappointed to find that Karl's will left everything, including the ranch, to Karl's children. Jonas was left out entirely.

Whether or not Jonas would have a claim against Karl's estate would depend on whether he could meet the conditions set out in law. They are the elements of resulting trust:

1. There must have been a specific promise made.

2. The promise must have been something that a reasonable person would believe.

3. The person to whom the promise was made must have taken steps to his or her own detriment because he or she relied on the promise.

4. The promise was not kept.

As with any type of estate litigation, you must prove all of the elements of the ground that you are relying on. You must prove all four of the above elements; if you fail to prove even one of them, your case will collapse. Let's look at these elements a little more closely to help you understand whether the facts of your case would support a claim of resulting trust.

1.1 Resulting trust element one: There must have been a specific promise made

The promise that was made to you must be specific. This does not necessarily mean that you must know exactly which words were said or on exactly which day they were said. This element refers to the fact that you must be able to identify the item or items that were promised and the conditions under which they would become yours. As an example, you must be able to prove that the promise made to you was for the quarter section of land on which the house is located, and not just a general promise that one day you would get some unidentified reward.

You must also be able to show that it was the deceased person who made the promise to you. It cannot have been something said by a third party who led you to believe that the promise had been made. You must have first-hand information from the deceased person.

If the promise was repeated numerous times, particularly in the hearing of several people, that is an important point in favour of someone wishing to establish this element. It shows that the promise originally made was not something the testator regretted saying. It wasn't something he was just joking about. Repeating his promise over time shows that he really meant it and he wanted you to know about it. It's also relevant if you can show that the promise was well known in the family as being the intention of the testator, as is often the case.

In the example used above, it is possible to identify that the item promised to Jonas was the farm belonging to Karl. The promise was made by Karl himself.

1.2 Resulting trust element two: Something that a reasonable person would believe

As you may have noticed, the law relies quite a bit on standards that refer to "a reasonable person." That standard applies here, too. The promise that was made to you must be something that makes sense in the context of your situation. For example, it would make sense if your father, who was a plumber, said that he would leave his plumbing business to you. It would not make sense for him to say that he would leave you a chalet in France and a villa in Portugal when you know full well he never owned any such properties.

The promise has to make sense, too. Would it make sense for your father to leave you his plumbing business if you are a hairdresser working in another province, while you have a sibling who is a plumber and is currently working with Dad in the family business? You must apply the test of whether that is a reasonable thing to believe. In other words, you have to use common sense when relying on a promise that was made to you.

In Jonas' case, the promise made sense because Karl's children had all said they didn't want the farm. Karl had expressed his desire to keep the farm in the family and had taken the time to train Jonas to run the farm.

1.3 Resulting trust element three: You must have taken steps to your detriment because of the promise

This is where most resulting trust claims fall apart, so take the time to consider this element very carefully. If the testator made a promise to you and that was the end of it, frankly the court will not care about the promise. If you did not make life choices or decisions because you relied on the promise, the court will not take the promise seriously. However, if you made decisions or took steps because you relied on that promise, and if those steps were to your detriment in some way, then all of a sudden, the promise matters. It will matter because of the concept of fairness. You might have made other choices for yourself if you had not believed that one day the testator would make good on the promise. If someone makes a promise to give you something and you act in a way that shows you are relying on that promise, then it is not fair for the person to renege on the promise.

Here are a few examples that demonstrate how you might rely on a promise to your own detriment:

- You might have been promised that one day you would own a particular building or piece of land. Relying on the promise, you might then put your own money into renovating, repairing, or improving that property. You would spend hours repairing fences, painting, and doing other physical labour. You would not have put your own money, time, and effort into it if you had known the promise would not be kept, so you have acted to your own detriment.

- You might have been promised that one day you would own the family business. You might then spend years working for next to no wages while you helped build the business into a thriving company. If you had known you would never own the company, you might have taken jobs elsewhere that paid more and stressed you out less. You would now be in a more secure financial situation.

- You might have been promised that if you moved in with your aging aunt to provide constant care, you would own her investments one day. Relying on that promise, you might move into a small room in her house in an inconvenient location. You might pass up job opportunities that would require moving away. You might pass up travel and a social life for many years and devote yourself to her daily comfort and care for no remuneration. If you had known

you would never receive the promised investments, you probably would not have done it.

As you can see, the essential part of this element is the fact that you must have done something significant that shows you relied on the promise and that you would be further ahead in some way (usually financially) if you had not relied on it. If you simply acknowledged the promise when it was made but never took any steps such as those discussed in the examples, then you have a very weak case for resulting trust.

Jonas took steps that showed he relied on Karl's promise. Jonas passed up the opportunity to go to university because he believed he already had a means of making a living. He devoted time, energy, and money to the farm that he would not have spent if he had not believed the farm would one day belong to him.

1.4 Resulting trust element four: The promise was not kept

The promise is broken when the person who makes the promise passes away and either made a will leaving the promised asset to someone else, or didn't make a will at all. In either event, you don't get the item you've been promised. Although it may be possible to claim resulting trust at other points in time such as upon the sale of a promised asset to someone else, we are discussing resulting trust in the context of estate litigation. Therefore we'll confine our discussion to promises that are broken when someone passes away.

2. What Happens to the Promised Asset when You Claim Resulting Trust?

If you are successful in claiming resulting trust, there are two general possibilities for what you will receive. One is that you may receive the actual item or piece of land that was promised to you. The other is that you might receive money as compensation instead of the actual asset. Don't go into your lawsuit assuming that if you win, you will automatically receive the property or the asset that is being litigated, or you might end up being very disappointed.

Whether or not you do receive the property in question will depend on several factors. The main factor will be whether the judge believes that monetary compensation is a reasonable substitute. This is because, as mentioned, the asset in question is usually land. Someone else will be living there, farming there, or otherwise making a living there. Taking the asset from that person and giving it to you would cause many other problems for several people. Therefore if at all possible, the judge will order that you receive money instead of the land. In order to receive the asset itself you would have to show that money simply could not replace it because of some unique factor of the asset.

3. Unjust Enrichment

Claims for resulting trust are often tied with claims for unjust enrichment. Either of these claims is perfectly capable of standing alone without the other, but the facts of many cases lead to them both being claimed at once. Whether you claim one or both remedies is up to you, as long as your claim is supported by the facts and the law. Remember though, that if you sue on one ground and lose, you may not have the opportunity to go back and try again on another ground so bundling your claims together may make sense strategically.

The basic idea of unjust enrichment is that somebody unfairly received a benefit that should have gone to you. The person was enriched by receiving something at your expense. As an example, you might have married someone who had been married before and had children from a previous marriage. You two lived in a home to which you contributed in terms of paying for numerous expenses and in general taking care of the house and yard. When your spouse died, he left the house you two lived in to his children from the first marriage. The property is in better shape than it would be if you had not looked after it, and the mortgage was paid off at least in part because you paid other bills, allowing your spouse to put more onto the mortgage.

In this example, the children who inherit the house might be unjustly enriched because of your efforts and bill payments, while you end up with nothing for all of that work. The reason it is unjust is that you did something to increase the value of an asset or create or preserve an asset and you lost out. Similar to resulting trust, it's a legal concept based on fairness.

The usual outcome of a successful claim for unjust enrichment is a monetary award. In other words, the court will try to put a dollar value on your loss and order the person who received the benefit to pay you that much money to compensate you for the loss. While that may sound like a simple concept, it is in fact extremely difficult. Many lawsuits take place simply over how to assess the value of the claim. These are the elements of unjust enrichment:

1. Someone received a benefit.

2. You suffered a loss that was connected to his or her benefit.

3. There was no juristic reason for the benefit to go to that beneficiary instead of to you.

3.1 Unjust enrichment element one: Someone received a benefit

Of the three elements of this ground, this is the easiest to establish. You can provide evidence that someone had been given a benefit by showing the will that left the asset to the beneficiary. It would be a good idea to take that one step further by showing that the beneficiary has actually taken possession of the asset left to him or her in the will.

3.2 Unjust enrichment element two: You suffered a loss that was connected to his or her benefit

To satisfy the second element, you must show that you suffered a loss and that your loss is somehow connected to the benefit received by another person. It is not enough just to show that one person received a piece of land and you did not. There is nothing legally unjust about giving different bequests to different people. It only becomes unfair — and therefore only becomes unjust enrichment — if their gain caused your loss.

The usual situation giving rise to a claim of unjust enrichment is that a person dies leaving a will that gives a benefit to a beneficiary at the expense of someone else. If you refer back to the earlier example of Karl's farm, you can see how Karl's children, who received the farm under Karl's will, benefited at Jonas' expense. Jonas increased the value and productivity of the farm at his own expense, so Karl's children received a farm that was worth more than it would have been worth without Jonas. Most likely, when Jonas claimed that the farm should be his based on Karl's promise, he would also claim that Karl's children were unjustly enriched at his expense.

In order to fit this scenario into the second element, you would show that Jonas's contributions to the farm only became his loss when the farm was left to other people. His loss is therefore directly connected to their gain.

3.3 Unjust enrichment element three: There was no juristic reason for the benefit to go to that beneficiary instead of you

This element is one of the more difficult principles you will have to deal with if you are bringing an unjust enrichment claim. "No juristic reason" means there was no reason according to law why that beneficiary should have received the benefit of receiving the bequest. This element has a two-part test, which you may think of as two hurdles to clear before you satisfy the element.

First you must deal with whether or not there is a juristic reason for that beneficiary to receive the bequest. Did the testator have a reason according to law for the bequest? This is important because a judge will want to know if that beneficiary had any right to the property (other than being left the property in the will). This step is all about understanding any existing rights of the beneficiary.

A juristic reason might be one of the following:

1. **A contract.** Perhaps the asset was left to the beneficiary because there was a legally binding agreement between the testator and the beneficiary that the asset was to go to him or her.

2. **An intention to donate.** The testator might have expressed an intention during his or her lifetime to donate the asset to a charitable organization.

3. **A statutory or common law requirement to leave that asset to someone else.** The testator might be legally required to give the asset to that other

person so that it wasn't his or hers to give to you. For example, the asset could be jointly owned by the testator and his or her spouse, meaning that the asset must go to that surviving joint owner.

If you are able to show that none of these reasons applies to your situation, you have cleared the first hurdle. The second step of the test is about you. You have to show that there is no legal reason why you are not entitled to receive the asset. The most common reason that a claimant is shown to have no right to the asset is a prenuptial or cohabitation agreement in which the claimant waived any right to receive the asset. Another possibility is that there is a lease in place which shows that the claimant is a tenant and therefore not entitled to share in the increase in value of the owner's property.

As part of the second step of this element, you must address the reasonable expectations of a person in your situation, taking all of the facts into consideration. As you can see, this element can quickly become complex. It can be particularly challenging when a couple lives together, during which time there are various economic benefits going to both parties on a continuous basis. It may be difficult to determine who paid more or who contributed more. The following is an example.

Susan and Francois lived in a common law marriage for 15 years. Susan died and left most of her estate, including her home, to her adult children from her previous marriage. Since she was the only one who made the mortgage payments, it seemed fair to her when she made her will that the house should be hers to do with as she wished. However, it didn't seem fair to Francois that he should receive nothing from the home. For the fifteen years that he had lived there, he had done all of the maintenance and repairs to the home, including painting inside and out, gardening, cleaning the eaves, building a deck, and replacing windows, saving Susan tens of thousands of dollars. He had paid for utilities, groceries, vacations, insurance, and pet care, freeing up her income to be used against the mortgage. Francois brought a claim for unjust enrichment, claiming that Susan's children benefited at his expense.

Situations such as that described for Susan and Francois are very common in estate litigation. In this case, the court would probably find that Francois was in fact entitled to a sum of money equivalent to some portion of the value of the house for his contributions by applying the two-part test discussed above.

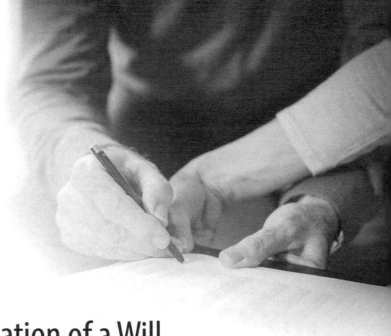

5

Clarification or Rectification of a Will

An application to clarify or rectify a will is a type of litigation that falls into the category of one that allows a will to stand. It is not designed to defeat or invalidate a will; in fact it is designed to help a will stay or become valid. Whether you are asking for clarification or rectification — two very different concepts — you are approaching the court to ask for help fixing an otherwise valid will so that the will can be saved.

1. Clarification of a Word, Phrase, or Term in a Will

Not every will is as clearly written as it should be. This happens particularly when a will is homemade, but not exclusively. There are some lawyer-made wills that contain mistakes, too. There may be a clause in the will that can be read two (or more) ways or something that is too vague to be helpful. Often there is a clause that mentions a group of people who are supposed to be beneficiaries

but it's not really clear who is in the group and who is not. There may be a reference to an asset but it is impossible to tell which asset is meant. In the really tough cases, there may be a clause that is completely meaningless. The purpose of a clarification application, also known as a construction or interpretation application, is to get a court ruling on what the testator meant by the problematic phrase in the will.

An executor doesn't have the legal authority to decide what ambiguous words in a will mean. Even if the executor did choose a meaning for unclear terms, there is going to be someone who is upset with his or her conclusion. The executor's job is to carry out the instructions in the will. If the instructions are not clear on the face of them, the executor needs clarification. Since the testator has passed away and is no longer around to explain what he or she meant, the only person who can decide the meaning of the words is a judge.

There are several aspects of clarification applications that are different from all other types of estate litigation. These unique aspects of clarification applications are:

1. Executors remain neutral and nobody is being sued.

2. Different paperwork.

3. Strict rules about outside evidence.

I will cover these aspects in the next sections.

1.1 Executors remain neutral and nobody is being sued

In applications for clarification of a will, the executor remains neutral on the subject of the question being asked of the court. It is unlike other lawsuits in which an executor takes a position and fights for it. In other lawsuits, the executor is suing someone or is being sued. In clarification applications, the executor is going as a neutral party to the court and asking for an interpretation of a word or phrase in the will so that the executor will know how to move forward with the estate. The executor simply asks the question and does not advocate for one interpretation or another.

In fact, it is considered very improper for an executor to take sides, so if you are bringing this type of application to the court, be sure to watch your phrasing in your documents. Be sure that you are asking what to do, and not suggesting to the court what you wish you could do.

Other parties may well become involved in the litigation once the executor begins it. A beneficiary who has a stake in the outcome will probably join the lawsuit and try to persuade the judge to give an interpretation that favours that beneficiary. Another stakeholder

in this type of claim might be a charitable organization who wants clarification on who shares the proceeds of a bequest, or a ruling on exactly what is in the bequest.

1.2 Different paperwork

Unlike all of the lawsuits and applications described in the other chapters of this book, a clarification application does not use a Statement of Claim to begin the lawsuit. It uses an Originating Notice instead. This notice will be described further in Chapter 8. The paperwork is different because you aren't suing anyone when you bring this lawsuit to court. You aren't claiming anything from anyone. It would be incorrect to name someone as a defendant (which is required under a Statement of Claim) because nobody is defending himself or herself against this lawsuit.

An Originating Notice achieves the same main goal as a Statement of Claim, which is to commence the lawsuit properly. There is a sample Originating Notice for each province in the download kit accompanying this book.

1.3 Strict rules about outside evidence

In most lawsuits discussed in this book, you will be allowed to use almost any evidence in your lawsuit as long as it is relevant to the issue at hand. You can use evidence from the lawyer who drew the will, from third parties, and even earlier statements of the deceased. An application for clarification is completely different from that; you can rarely introduce any evidence other than the will itself. Any evidence that is not in the will itself is referred to as extrinsic evidence.

The reason for the strict rules that keep out evidence is the concept of what the court is trying to achieve, which is to understand what the will actually says and what it means. The idea is for the judge to read the will and try to understand the mind and intention of the testator without resorting to outside information. This is known as the "armchair rule" because the idea is for the judge to sit, figuratively, in the testator's chair, understand all of the circumstances of which he testator would have been aware at the time, and think like the testator.

This is a difficult concept to work with in terms of preparing for your hearing, partly because there is not much help to be found from precedent cases. Every will is different, as is every testator and every situation. Therefore it's really difficult to find precedent cases that will help guide you as to what evidence to bring.

Here are more detailed explanations of the general rules about what you can and cannot do in a clarification application:

1. **The application is being brought because there is a word or a clause that is problematic.** However, the judge must look at the entire will and not just the problematic clause. The rest of the will gives context to the problematic phrase. If you bring a lawsuit for clarification of a word or phrase, remember that it must be read as part of a larger document; don't isolate the phrase and try to understand it without the rest of the will as its foundation.

2. **When a judge is attempting to clarify a will, the intent is to clarify what is actually there in the document.** If at all possible, this should be done without bringing in outside evidence. In other words, the best solution is for the document to speak for itself without relying on outside information to make sense of it. This principle is known as the Limited Extrinsic Evidence Rule.

3. **The judge must interpret the words in the will on their plain meanings.** The judge cannot rely on words that are not there or ignore words that are there. The judge has to look at what the testator did write in his will, not what he meant to write or might have said he intended to write. If you want the judge to add or remove words to give meaning to what the testator put in the will, you are bringing the wrong kind of lawsuit. Adding or removing words can only be done in the context of a rectification application, which will be covered later in this chapter.

4. **You cannot bring any evidence about what the testator intended to write.** This means that you cannot get the lawyer who drafted the will to give evidence about what the testator instructed for his will. The judge can only go by what actually is in the will.

5. **To give a framework to the clarification of the will, the judge should consider any circumstances that were known to the testator at the time the will was made.** The judge should know all about the testator's family and finances so that he or she can place himself or herself in the testator's place and see the will through the testator's eyes. Therefore if you are bringing this type of application, you should expect to provide that kind of evidence in affidavit form in chambers, and by oral testimony if it goes to a trial.

6. **You cannot bring any evidence about assets that the testator obtained after he or she wrote the will.** This is because at the time the will was made, the testator didn't have those assets and therefore could not have intended to dispose of them in the will.

7. **The judge must consider what the testator knew on the day the will was made, not on the day the testator died.**

2. Exceptions to the "Limited Extrinsic Evidence" Rules

As with most rules, this one has an exception. In fact there are two exceptions, or two situations in which you are allowed to bring in outside evidence. Before you can bring this evidence, there will have to be a hearing in chambers for a judge to agree that there is a need for the exception and to permit you to give the evidence.

2.1 Exception one

You may bring evidence that helps the court identify an object or asset referred to in the will, if the question for the court is to figure out what asset is being given away.

2.2 Exception two

If the question for the court is to identify a beneficiary or a group of beneficiaries, you will be allowed to bring evidence about the people who claim they are beneficiaries. This is necessary in order for the judge to understand who was in the testator's life at the time he or she made the will, and to understand their circumstances. This means you will be able to give information about their ages, relationship to the deceased, living arrangements when the will was made, finances, and many other facts.

With both of these exceptions, you must be extremely careful about the evidence you bring because making a mistake might result in your application being thrown out and you having to start all over with a different kind of application. For example, if you bring in evidence that there was a mistake in the will,

you have all of a sudden changed your application from a clarification application to a rectification application. If you bring evidence of fraud or forgery, you have caused your application to change from a clarification to a will challenge. This matters because, as you can see from reading this book, the rules, forms, and processes are different depending on the kind of application you are bringing. You cannot just change direction midstream.

3. Rectification of a Will

In general terms, rectifying a will means fixing an error in a will. This type of application is often misunderstood because many people believe they can use it as a way of making changes to a will they don't particularly like. However, the whole point of rectification applications is to ensure that the intentions of the testator are not lost or skewed because of a mistake made by the person who drafted the will. In other words, this type of application is meant to fix mistakes by the lawyer or drafter, and not mistakes that someone believes the testator may have made.

In rectification applications there is usually a will that on the face of it looks absolutely fine, has been executed properly, and in every way appears to be valid. However, there is a mistake in the will that is made in the production of the document itself and should not mean that the intentions of the testator are void.

Canadian courts will consider rectifying wills only if one of the following situations exists:

1. There is a typo or clerical error that affects the meaning of the will.

2. The instructions given by the testator to the lawyer were not understood by

the person who drafted the will and therefore were not properly set out in the will.

3. The instructions given by the testator were understood by the drafter and addressed in the will but were not properly set out in the will.

You will note that the above situations do not say anything about the testator making a mistake or not understanding the will. You cannot rectify a will on the basis that the testator didn't understand it; that would instead be an application for lack of mental capacity or for lack of knowledge and approval of the contents.

If the court is going to rectify a will, it does so by adding or deleting words to the existing will. The judge does not make decisions about who is going to get what; he or she will simply correct the mistake on the face of the will and then give the executor the go-ahead to carry on with the revised will.

3.1 What do I have to prove?

In a rectification application, you must obtain an affidavit from the lawyer who drafted the will, or the student-at-law or staff member who drafted the will. The affidavit must explain how the mistake happened. For example, was an assistant preparing a will from notes that were illegible? Did the drafting lawyer mean to come back and re-draft a section of the will but then forget to do so? The people who prepared the will are the only ones who know exactly what happened so their evidence in the form of an affidavit is absolutely essential.

The court will consider your request to rectify the will if your evidence shows the following:

1. When the entire will is read, it is clear from reading it that a mistake has occurred in the drafting of the will.

2. The existence of the mistake means that the will does not accurately or completely express the testator's intentions as determined from the will as a whole.

3. The words used throughout the will as a whole make it so obvious what the testator intended to do that it makes no sense for the testator to have meant what the mistake says.

4. Correcting the mistake so that it shows the testator's real intentions can be achieved by deleting words or adding words or both.

5. Once the mistake is corrected, it will make sense when reading the whole will and looking at the surrounding circumstances.

Here is an example:

Marcia always intended to treat all four of her children equally in her will. This is how she dealt with them throughout their lives because she believed it to be the fair way of doing things. When she met with her lawyer, Marcia mentioned this wish to treat all her children equally and the lawyer made note of it. Later, the lawyer dictated the will to his assistant, who prepared the will according to the lawyer's instructions. The lawyer included in the will a clause instructing that the house be sold and divided equally among all four children, and another dividing the contents of the home equally among the children. Unfortunately, while the lawyer was dictating the clause about the residue of the estate, he had only listed three of the children's names when he was interrupted by a telephone call. He returned to the will a few minutes later but forgot to add the fourth child's name. Neither the lawyer nor Marcia noticed the mistake when the will was signed. After Marcia passed away, her executor contacted the lawyer to try to understand why the fourth child was left out of the residue clause and as a result, the mistake came to light. The executor asked the judge to fix the mistake and the lawyer provided an affidavit explaining that his error meant that Marcia's wishes were not fully expressed in her will.

You will note that in the list of what you have to prove, the instructions refer to looking at the will "as a whole." This means that you cannot choose a single line or phrase out of context. It has to be clear when looking at the entire will that the line or phrase seems out of place. In the example of Marcia and the child who was omitted, it would have been clear from reading the rest of the will that Marcia had intended the residue of the estate to go to all of her children.

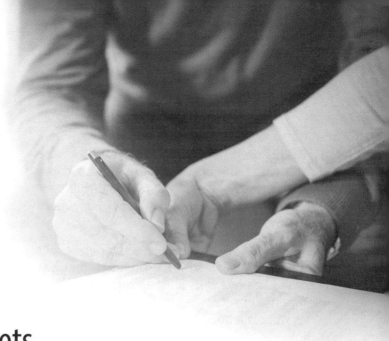

6

Ownership of Joint Assets

One of the most common do-it-yourself estate planning moves made by Canadians happens when a parent or grandparent adds a child, niece, nephew, or grandchild to the title of a bank account or home. It is widely known among lawyers that this is a disastrous move in the vast majority of cases, but still Canadians continue to take this step. In most cases, they do so without legal advice and never find out how big the mistake is; their families pay the price after the parents or grandparents have passed away.

Adding someone to your home, cabin, or bank accounts is easy to do, cheap, and quick. Furthermore, there is a popular misconception among the population that it is an effective way to avoid probate, reduce probate fees, and generally make estate administration easier. It rarely works as planned. Instead, the result is a mess. There are endless disputes based on the adding of a name to an asset. Removing a name from an asset is extremely difficult. This is because it is so

easy to talk about "adding" a name when in reality, adding that name means you are giving a person legal rights to your assets. Legal rights cannot be taken away from someone just because you have second thoughts.

In fact, litigation regarding joint assets is so prevalent these days that this book will devote this entire chapter to it as a subset of estate litigation. This chapter will look at joint real property as well as joint financial assets.

1. Joint Ownership

The distinguishing hallmark of joint ownership of an asset is that, usually, there is full ownership by right of survivorship. This means that when there are two joint owners and one of them dies, the other one — the survivor — has the right to keep the entire asset. The same rule applies when there are three or four or any number of owners. As each one passes away, the others absorb his or her share until finally only one person is left standing. That person owns the asset.

That person can then sell or give away the asset, or leave it to someone in his or her will.

This used to be how all joint assets were dealt with. Now, as you will see in this chapter, the rules have changed. Not all joint assets go to the survivor anymore. This is where the litigation comes in.

Part of the reason that litigation about joint accounts is so widespread is that everyone has heard of joint accounts and joint property, but very few people actually know the details about how it works. There are thousands of articles and webpages in our country and in others that warn readers of the horrors of probate and urge them to avoid probate at all costs. Putting assets into joint names with the adult children is often touted as a great solution to avoiding probate, based on the concept that the child will outlive the parent, and the child will then peacefully sell the house and divide the funds fairly among his or her siblings as the parent had actually wanted.

In real life, nothing works that smoothly. There are many ways joint assets can be disastrous for the parent while the parent is still alive, as well as when the parent dies. If there is an asset in joint names with one of the children, chances are very good that the child will claim that he or she is supposed to own the house alone and not share it with siblings. In some cases, the child assumes or believes this to be the parent's intention. In other cases the child knows full well it's not the parent's intention that he or she keep the house but feels legally safe keeping it based on the concept of joint property ownership and the right of survivorship.

Because of the risks to the parents and the huge losses to estates because of misused joint assets, adding a child or grandchild's name to an asset is now considered one of the most widely used methods of financially abusing a vulnerable parent or grandparent. The ease, speed, privacy, and low cost of adding a name to an asset makes it a popular way of stealing assets from a parent. All of this background is provided to explain why we now have rules in place that disallow joint assets from going to the surviving child, and how the rules are supposed to work during estate litigation.

1.1 Does the jointly owned asset belong to the estate or the survivor?

In some circumstances, jointly owned assets still go to the surviving joint owner. For example, accounts held jointly by spouses or common law partners will still belong to the person who outlives the other.

In other circumstances, the jointly owned asset does not go to the surviving joint owner. Those circumstances arise when a person of one generation, say a parent, grandparent, aunt or uncle, add a younger person such as an adult child, a grandchild, a niece, or a nephew, to a bank account or a house title. As discussed above, this arrangement is often made without legal advice and without much guidance, and many readers will recognize this arrangement from their own families. Do not assume that in these circumstances the asset belongs to the younger person when the older one dies. In fact, you should assume the opposite.

A joint account or joint title belongs to the person who died and NOT the surviving joint owner if all of these conditions are met:

1. An older person added someone, usually a family member from a younger generation, to an asset. A variation on the situation arises when instead of a younger family member, a caregiver is added, but that situation is less common.

2. The asset belonged to the older person first, and the younger person did not contribute to the funds or help purchase the title.

3. The younger person was added to help the older person with banking, for convenience, to avoid probate, to reduce probate fees, or for some other reason that has nothing to do with the older person wanting the younger person to own the asset.

If all of these conditions are met, the presumption of resulting trust kicks in. This means the law presumes the asset is held by the younger person in trust for the estate of the older person. The asset does not belong to the younger person. See Checklist 2 to determine whether the asset you are dealing with is presumed to belong to the estate or not.

At that point, the younger person should turn over the asset to the estate. If that happens, there is no legal issue. However, the younger person may believe that he or she is the true owner of the joint asset and should own the asset after the death of the older person. This is the point at which lawsuits take place with respect to joint assets. The vast majority of litigation surrounding jointly owned property involves a fight over who owns the asset.

2. The Executor's Position

If the executor has determined that someone is holding an asset that really belongs to the estate and cannot persuade that person to hand over the asset voluntarily, the executor will have to try to compel the return of the asset by suing the person holding the asset. An executor does not have the authority

CHECKLIST 2
TO WHOM DOES THE JOINTLY OWNED ASSET ACTUALLY BELONG?

Use this checklist to determine whether the asset you are concerned with fits the description of a jointly owned asset that does not belong to the surviving joint owner.

1. [   ] Is the joint ownership between people of different generations, such as a mother and son, a grandfather and grandson, or an aunt and a niece?

2. [   ] Was the account or the land originally that of the older person, with the younger person being added to the ownership of the asset later?

3. [   ] If the asset in question is a bank account or investment, did the younger person not contribute any of the money?

4. [   ] Was the younger person's name added so that he or she could help the older person with banking or finances?

5. [   ] Was the younger person's name added to a house or cabin so that the family could avoid going through the court probate process?

6. [   ] Whose idea was it to add the younger person's name to the asset?

If the answer to questions 1 through 5 is YES, it is very likely the jointly owned asset may not actually belong to the survivor.

to decide to allow a joint asset to be kept by someone else if it belongs to the estate. An executor who does so should expect the beneficiaries who would have received the asset to sue the executor for the value of the asset.

If the executor is also a person who is a surviving joint owner of an asset held jointly with the deceased, this may well be a conflict of interest. If the executor puts the asset into the estate, all is well. If the executor asserts that he or she is the rightful owner of the asset, he or she should renounce as executor due to conflict of interest.

3. Undue Influence

Lawsuits dealing with ownership of joint property are often combined with lawsuits alleging undue influence. This is because it often appears to family members that the property or the bank account was only put into joint names because a parent was influenced into doing so. As was said at the beginning of the chapter, this is quite often the case; it happens every day that someone convinces a parent to add a name to an asset. In most cases, the child whose name was put on the joint asset may also be getting the largest share of the estate.

If the facts of your case seem to support undue influence as the reason for adding the name to the asset in the first place and you are challenging the will as well, the best idea is to use undue influence as the ground for the challenge to the will. In your Statement of Claim and Affidavit in Support, include your allegation that the undue influence was not confined to the will but also extended to the name being added to the asset.

This does not mean that you must challenge the will itself in order to challenge the ownership of the joint asset. If the facts of your case support that, then that is the route

to take. On the other hand, if the will itself seems fine and there is no need to challenge it, then your lawsuit should be only about the joint asset. You will file the Statement of Claim, serve it in the usual way, then appear in chambers to advise the judge about what is going on and to set a trial date.

4. The Evidence Needed

This lawsuit is all about establishing the intent of the deceased older person. The executor is the plaintiff and the person refusing to give up the asset is the defendant.

When a certain arrangement of facts exist, as discussed in this chapter, there is a presumption that the asset belongs to the estate. In order to keep the asset, the defendant must overcome or rebut the presumption. There is only one effective way to do so, and that is to come up with evidence of the intentions of the deceased older person. The evidence must have been made around the time the asset was put into joint names and must have come from the deceased joint owner. In addition, the evidence must have direct relevance to the issue of whether the deceased joint owner wanted the younger joint owner to own the property for himself or herself to keep, or wanted the younger one to distribute the asset to other people.

While it's true that the defendant wants to find such evidence, it is in your interests to find it as well. If you are able to locate some definitive proof of what the deceased joint owner wanted to do with the asset, not only may you win your lawsuit, but you may be able to settle it without having to resort to a court battle in the first place.

If it seems that such evidence is difficult to come by, you are correct. Not many people tend to leave written evidence of why they took certain steps when they have no idea that taking such steps is going to be problematic in the future. Depending on the type of asset you are dealing with, you might find some of these suggestions helpful in finding some evidence of the deceased's intent:

1. Check for a clause in the will that deals with the joint asset.

2. If a lawyer drew up the deceased's will, check to see whether there are any notes about the asset in question.

3. Check for any other documentation signed by the older person that deals with assets, such as a family trust or bare trust. These are not do-it-yourself documents so likely would be in the possession of a lawyer.

4. In the case of a joint bank account, check with the bank personnel to see whether they took any notes on the day the joint account was set up. This also goes for any funds held with a money manager or financial advisor.

5. Also ask bank personnel if they have any personal recollection of a discussion with the deceased about the joint ownership.

6. If a lawyer was involved in transferring the title to land, ask whether there is anything in his or her notes about why the land was transferred.

7. Talk to people in the family to find out whether the deceased joint owner talked to anyone about his or her intentions for the property or why it was put into joint names.

The decision about who legally owns joint assets will be made only after a full trial has been held so that all parties can give evidence before a trial judge. If the judge decides that the asset belongs to the estate, the executor will need to distribute that asset along with everything else in the will.

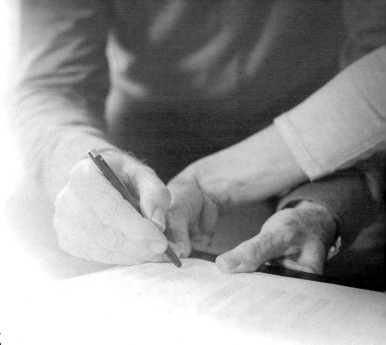

7
Chambers Applications

1. Our Court System

Some information about the structure of the court system will help clarify where you are and what you're doing if you are bringing an application to chambers, also known as justice's chambers. Each province and territory in Canada has two court systems; they are the provincial court and the superior court. The provincial courts differ across the country in some respects but generally speaking they handle family law (child custody, child maintenance, visitation rights), traffic, small claims court, and less serious criminal charges.

The superior court is called either the Supreme Court or the Court of Queen's Bench, depending on which province you live in. The superior court system handles more serious criminal charges as well as civil (i.e., non-criminal) trials of all kinds. This court also handles appeals from decisions made in provincial court and in administrative tribunals. The most important fact for the subject matter of this book is that the superior court handles all probate- and wills-related matters.

If a decision made in the superior court is appealed, it goes to the court of appeal for that province. That is the highest court in any province or territory. The only higher court available after that is the Supreme Court of Canada, the highest court in our country at a federal, rather than provincial level.

Estate litigation is all done within the superior court of the province or territory. When there is a trial going on, a specific judge and a specific courtroom are assigned to it. Only the people and staff involved in that trial are generally present because the court's time and attention have been reserved for that particular trial.

However, there are dozens of lawyers and individuals who need a few minutes of a judge's time for help with advice on how to proceed, emergency situations, or with matters that may take an hour or two to discuss.

None of those matters is a full trial, but these matters still need the attention of a judge. It could be for five minutes or an hour. These matters are heard and decided by a justice (which is the proper name for a judge of the superior court) sitting in chambers. Though this may sound like a cozy office setting, it is in reality an open courtroom.

In smaller cities, there may be only one or two justices sitting in chambers on any given day and chambers may not even be running every weekday. In larger cities, there are several chambers courtrooms open at once. Usually each courtroom has a list, or docket, of the different cases that people have alerted the court they are going to bring to the judge that day. Larger cities may have as many as 40 or 50 items on a daily chambers docket. You have to arrange in advance, in accordance with the Rules of Court, to have your case called on any particular day. (We'll go into those arrangements a little later in this book.) As you can see, the chambers system is designed to give you access to the superior court when you need it.

A chambers judge will hear and decide on a huge variety of matters. On any given day, the judge might hear everything from two lawyers adjourning an application to give their clients time to negotiate, to a dispute about whether one of the parties to the lawsuit was given the proper notice of the hearing. If the issue you are raising in front of the judge is expected to take 20 minutes or longer, in some jurisdictions you may have to go to special chambers.

As you guide your lawsuit through the court system, you are very likely to have at least one or two visits to ask a chambers judge for assistance. If your lawsuit gets all the way to a trial, that will be held in a trial courtroom with a trial judge, which is very different from chambers. Everything short of a full trial will be held in chambers. Most of the time, the application you make to the judge is an interlocutory application, meaning that it's happening within the course of your lawsuit. In other words, the help you need or the question you are going to ask the judge has something to do with your lawsuit but is not the final, full trial. For example, you could ask the judge to compel the people on the other side of the lawsuit to file a document within a certain time frame.

In other cases, the chambers judge is going to make a decision that ends the lawsuit. In terms of estate matters, this is often the case. This is because the application is for a passing of executor's accounts or to determine the ownership of a specific asset or similar questions. These things can be decided without a full trial.

Chambers is less formal than a trial courtroom in terms of the procedures and even the deportment of the lawyers. You do not call witnesses to the stand and you don't cross-examine anyone. However, you will be expected to conduct yourself with the utmost good manners and courtesy in the courtroom, even if you are not the one speaking. Do not interrupt the judge or anyone from an opposing party who may be speaking. Stand up when it's your turn to speak and talk only to the judge, not to the other parties in the courtroom. Do not use foul or abusive language. Turn off your cell phone. Dress in business attire if possible. Do not address the judge as "your honour," as that is reserved for provincial court. You may address the judge as "justice" or as "my lord" or "my lady." If all else fails, calling the judge "sir" or "madam" is still respectful.

Giving evidence in chambers is much different than giving evidence in a trial. You will need time to prepare the necessary evidence, as chambers evidence is given in the form of written, sworn affidavits. Before approaching or starting anything in chambers, be sure to read Chapter 9 about giving evidence and Chapter 10 about preparing your affidavit evidence so that you are properly prepared.

In this chapter, we are going to discuss some chambers applications that are unique to estates and are some of the most common lawsuits involving estates. Though this chapter does not by any means include every possible matter that could go to chambers, you may well see your potential lawsuit discussed here.

2. Removal of an Executor

An application in chambers that many beneficiaries want to make is for the removal of an executor who was named by a will. Almost every beneficiary who is unhappy with some aspect of an estate or a distribution at some time thinks about asking the court to remove the executor. I field this question several times a week. Though it sounds simple, an application to remove an executor is anything but simple; it is an uphill battle.

The main reason these applications are not easy to win is that the person who passed away made his or her choice of who should be his or her executor. The court will do everything it reasonably can to uphold the wishes of the deceased person. The court won't simply remove an executor because of a small mistake or delay, or because you think someone else would do a better job.

This means that in order to succeed in a request to remove an executor, you will have to show the court that the executor is behaving in such a way that he or she is endangering or wasting the estate, or in a way that is not in the best interests of the estate. There

are plenty of rules that are intended to ensure that an executor manages the estate properly, but executors are human too and sometimes they don't do things as well as they should. Executors are generally not removed for making a single mistake when they acted in good faith.

If the executor told you that you would receive your cheque in a week but then didn't deliver it to you for ten days, that is not a big enough mistake for the judge to remove an executor. You would be wasting your time and money taking something like that to court. On the other hand, if the executor took the cash in the estate and paid off all his or her own bills or you found out that several thousand dollars somehow just disappeared and cannot be explained, then you have something to go on. If you think the executor is taking too long because it has been six months since someone passed away, you are probably too impatient. However, if it has been six years, there is definitely something wrong.

It's a matter of degree; was the action by the executor unforgivable, or was it just inconvenient for you? Is the executor dishonest or do you simply not like the way he or she does things? There is no litmus test that applies to everyone because the circumstances vary so widely from one estate to another.

If you are considering making an application to remove an executor, it might be a good idea to see a lawyer to get an opinion on the strength of your case or to do some research about the role of an executor. I suggest this simply because many people think they understand what an executor is supposed to do when in reality they do not. The role is very poorly understood. There are many beneficiaries who let their dislike of the executor heighten their dissatisfaction and they lose perspective. Still others just want to be the one in charge and cannot or will not accept that someone else was appointed. In other words, there seems to be an enormous amount of misinformation out there about what executors are supposed to do and how beneficiaries are supposed to deal with them. This leads to pointless lawsuits that cannot succeed.

A second reason that it is difficult to remove an executor is that there are other options the court may consider appropriate. These would be options that would help the estate move along properly and ease the concerns of the beneficiaries. Here is an example:

Noel applied to the court to remove the executor of his mother's estate. The executor was Noel's sister, Ann Marie. Noel had a number of complaints about how Ann Marie was handling the estate, but his main problem was that Ann Marie would not list their mother's house for sale. She kept putting it off, saying she wasn't emotionally up to cleaning out the house yet. While Ann Marie was delaying, the estate was paying for the property tax, insurance, and electrical bill for the house even though nobody was living there. The house had now been vacant for a year. Noel explained to the judge that Ann Marie was not acting in the best interest of the estate by refusing to get on with the sale and that he wanted Ann Marie removed so that he could take over. Ann Marie opposed Noel's lawsuit and insisted that as executor she had the right to list the house when she thought it best to do so. Instead of granting either Noel's or Ann Marie's request, the judge ordered Ann Marie to have the house cleaned out and listed on the market within 30 days.

In this case, the court found a solution that preserved the mother's decision that Ann Marie should be in charge as well as resolved Noel's concern about the delay in selling the house. It's important to realize that you may not get exactly what you ask for in court. The people on the other side of the argument — in this case, Ann Marie — might not get what they want either. The judge has the power to come up with creative solutions that you haven't even thought about or asked for.

3. What Happens If Nobody Can Agree on Anything?

In a good number of requests for removal of an executor, it becomes apparent that the parties are simply never going to get along under any circumstances. The war between executors and beneficiaries can become extraordinarily bitter and vicious. The court application dissolves into a nasty exchange of insults and allegations that is not about legal rights or principles anymore; by then it's just a brawl between angry siblings. When this happens, the court will realize that allowing the executor to continue means that every step of the estate is going to be a prolonged and wasteful battle. Each side is going to make life impossible for the other. Obviously the court has to intervene because the parties are beyond making any headway themselves. If the judge doesn't take steps, the estate is going to be wasted on legal fees and nobody is ever going to see their inheritance.

It's important to realize that when things get to this point, it is very rare that a judge will pick any of the feuding parties to be the executor in place of the current executor. There is still going to be a stalemate when the same parties are involved in the same issue so nothing is gained by granting a request to remove one sibling and replace him or her with another. In cases like this, the court will, most of the time, remove the current executor and appoint the Office of the Public Trustee in his or her place. The Public Trustee is neutral and has experience in estate administration so the courts are usually confident that the estate is in better hands once removed from the feuding parties and given to the Public Trustee.

It is also possible in a battle like this over executorship that the court might appoint a trust company instead of the Public Trustee, depending on the facts of the case and in particular the size or value of the estate. Like the Public Trustee, a trust company is a neutral third party who will treat all members of the family and all of the beneficiaries equally. They will carry out the will without any personal feelings interfering with the job.

4. What Do I Have to Prove?

If you are applying to remove an executor, the onus is on you to prove there is a really good reason to remove him or her. Though of course the executor will defend himself or herself against your accusations, you are the one who must make the case. Here is a list of what you must show the court:

1. The executor has failed in one of the fundamental duties of an executor, which are:

   a. Duty to act in the best interest of the estate.

   b. Duty to follow the instructions in the will.

   c. Duty to maximize and protect estate assets.

   d. Duty to act honestly and in good faith.

   e. Duty to remain neutral among beneficiaries.

   f. Duty to distribute the estate in a timely manner.

2. The failure on the part of the executor — which is usually referred to as a breach of the executor's duties — is serious enough that if the executor is allowed to carry on, there is a real danger to the estate.

The cases that deal with this area of law clarify for us what kind of behaviour or situation might lead to a removal of the executor and what will not. Here are some of the factors that will not be enough to remove an executor appointed by a will:

1. A single mistake made in good faith.

2. Hostility or friction between the executor and the beneficiary.

3. A suspicion that the executor might not carry out the estate properly, as opposed to an action already taken or a pattern of behaviour already established by the executor.

It is worth noting that in recent years, judges have been punishing beneficiaries and executors alike for bringing lawsuits that are not really serious enough to need the court's assistance. In many of the cases heard in court, judges have expressed the opinion that adults should behave like adults and work out matters between them if they possibly can. When a judge believes that a lawsuit has been brought for malicious reasons (such as embarrassing someone, causing them pain or trauma, or upsetting them), the judge may order costs against the party who is behaving that way. This is why, throughout this book, I have repeatedly said that it's important to examine your motivation.

5. Passing of Accounts

Another application that is made frequently in chambers is for the passing of the executor's accounts. Passing of accounts refers to a process in which a judge looks at the financial accounts prepared by an executor and decides whether they are acceptable in terms of accuracy and completeness. The accounts refers to a record of all of the transactions an executor has handled from the day he or she started acting as executor until a stated end date. Most executors prepare the accounts themselves but others will hire an accountant or bookkeeper, depending on the complexity of the material and the number of entries that need to be handled. Either method is acceptable.

A passing of accounts application can be an application on its own or it might be combined with other requests. For example, if you are applying to remove an executor, you will also want that executor to pass his or her accounts before leaving the job.

There is no single form of accounts that is required in all jurisdictions, but their purpose and scope are the same everywhere. The idea is to give a summary of the estate's finances from the first day until the present using a group of documents. All executors' accounts will have certain elements in common, as follows:

1. The inventory that was prepared after the death of the testator. The inventory is supposed to give a snapshot of the financial situation of the deceased on the very day that he or she died. Executors don't always get this right because they don't understand the significance of getting the balances on the date of death. The inventory establishes a starting point. This is the point at which the assets stopped belonging to the deceased and became part of his or her estate, and therefore became the responsibility of the executor.

2. The ledger. This is a statement that shows in detail every single transaction undertaken by the executor since the day the testator passed away. All funds coming into the estate, such as proceeds of the sale of the house or the money earned as interest on term deposits, show up on the ledger going into the estate. All funds going out, such as payment of bills or distributions to beneficiaries, are shown as funds going out of the estate. While it is acceptable for an executor to give beneficiaries a summarized accounting for the purpose of getting a release from the beneficiaries, when it comes to litigation the summary will no longer be enough. On a passing of accounts application to court, every single item must be accounted for and explained. The ledger is the simplest and most effective way to provide all of that information because it is a simple format, it is in chronological order, and it is easy for anyone looking at it to find specific items.

As you can likely see, it would be essential to have a full accounting if the executor was being removed or was voluntarily stepping down from the job. Without a good accounting, you would not know whether a certain transaction had been managed by the old executor or the new one. That could become extremely important if the transaction in question turned out to be fraudulent or negligent. You need to know who was in charge when any particular step was taken.

5.1 Who can apply to pass executors' accounts?

The application for passing of accounts is interesting because of the fact that it can be brought either by the executor or by the beneficiaries. It's pretty unusual in litigation that opposing parties want to bring the same application. Most of the time, an application by one party would be detrimental to the other. However, that is exactly what happens with passing of accounts applications because either side can request it to break a stalemate. A passing of accounts application may take place at any time during an estate. It is not always done at the end or just when an executor is leaving. It is the go-to application for beneficiaries to bring when they cannot get enough information from a hostile or reluctant executor. It is often brought by the executors themselves if beneficiaries are being unreasonable and will not approve his or her accounts.

If you are a beneficiary who is bringing an application to pass the executor's accounts, the onus is on you to show that there is something wrong with the accounts. This cannot be a blanket assumption that "something is wrong." The court will not allow a fishing expedition of that sort. You must be able to point out specific transactions on specific days, or to point out that a certain asset is missing. For example, you might point out that the deceased had two GICs before he died but only one shows on the accounting. You have to be able to identify specific problems.

You must also be prepared to describe to the judge the efforts you made to get the information you need about the accounts or to get your questions answered by the executor. Obviously nobody should commence a court action for a passing of accounts without having tried to resolve the issues with the executor first. Your affidavit should include copies of the letters or emails you sent to the executor asking about missing items or wrong amounts. You may also tell the court about telephone calls or texts you made to the executor for the same purpose. It's important for you to demonstrate that you made every reasonable effort to work with the executor on the accounts before resorting to the court.

You will have to show that the executor is being obstructive, belligerent, secretive, or simply unresponsive to your inquiries.

If you are an executor applying to the court to pass your own accounts, you will have to explain why you are proceeding through the court and not through the normal procedure of having the beneficiaries review and sign off on the accounts by signing a release. It is not unusual for an executor to apply to pass his or her accounts and there will be no stigma attached to your application by the court. However, you will have to show the court that regular communication broke down and the usual method of having the beneficiaries approve your accounting was not available to you.

In general, an executor will want to show the court the following:

1. The records are complete and accurate.

2. There are reasonable, documented explanations for anything in the accounts that, on the face of it, looks unusual.

3. No funds or assets are missing, damaged, wasted, or improperly valued.

4. The executor has acted honestly and in good faith with estate assets.

5. The executor has responded to reasonable inquiries for more information.

6. The beneficiaries are being unreasonable in their demands or in their refusal to participate in the estate process.

7. It's in the best interests of the estate to pass the accounts.

6. Procedural Questions

An executor or a beneficiary may ask the court for advice or assistance when a matter of procedure is unclear or they run into roadblocks when following the normal procedure. For example, there may be a beneficiary named in the will who has no fixed address and the executor does not know how to let the beneficiary know about matters going ahead in court. The executor might want the court's permission to serve notice on the beneficiary in a way not normally allowed, such as sending a copy to the beneficiary's parents.

Other requests could be for extensions of time allowed for taking certain steps, for setting down a trial date, or for clarification of who should be given notice of a hearing. On any given chambers day, the justice will hear several of these matters from various parties who just need a bit of guidance or authority to keep their cases moving along. In most jurisdictions, you can give opposing parties as little as two days' notice for this kind of brief appearance in court.

7. Preliminary Matters before Trial

When there is a trial held in court, there is a lot of work that happens in and out of the courtroom before the trial takes place. There are often several chambers applications that lead up to the trial itself. Some of these applications are purely procedural. However, many of them are more substantial and may take hours or even days of chambers court time to resolve.

For example, in Chapter 2 we looked at challenging a will on the ground of undue influence. As described in that chapter, in order to get a trial date on a challenge on undue influence, first you must have a chambers hearing in which the person who has objected to the will has the responsibility of showing that suspicious circumstances existed at the time the will was made. This kind of hearing might well take a few days to complete, depending on the number of witnesses and the amount of factual information to get through.

8

How to Get Your Lawsuit into Court

Many Canadians are familiar with small claims court and perhaps assume that launching a lawsuit regarding an estate will be similar. They are actually not similar lawsuits at all. You will find the process of contesting a will much more complicated and time-consuming. Do not try to use small claims forms to start or conduct your lawsuit as they will not be accepted by the court. Not only are wills and estates forms different from small claims court, but the process is different too. The higher court is not set up to be user-friendly to non-lawyers the way small claims court is. There are not a lot of people appearing in the higher courts without lawyers and it may feel somewhat disorienting to be the only non-lawyer in the courtroom.

1. First Step: Statement of Claim

To begin your lawsuit, you must file a Statement of Claim. This document identifies the parties to the lawsuit, the court in which it is going to be heard, and the issue that is being disputed. (The download that accompanies this book has a form of Statement of Claim for each province and territory.) The person who starts a lawsuit by filing a Statement of Claim is known as the plaintiff. The person or people who are being sued are known as defendants. "Filing" your Statement of Claim means that you prepare it, sign it, and take it to the Clerk of the Probate Court at the courthouse. Make sure to make a copy of your Statement of Claim because the court is going to keep your original document.

Once your Statement of Claim has been filed with the court registry, it is given a court file number and you will pay a fee. Table 4 sets out the fee for each province and territory. On the day you file your documents, make note of your file number when it is assigned by the clerk because you will use it many times. Once you have filed the Statement of Claim and it has a court file number, anything else the court receives from any party that has to do with that lawsuit gets the same court file number (also sometimes called an action number). Think of your Statement of Claim as the front cover of a book. All of the pages within the book are the interlocutory matters that take place under that cover before you get to the end of the book, which is the trial.

Any time you call, email, or visit the courthouse or registry to ask a question about your file, you must refer to the court file number.

1.1 An exception to the rule: The Originating Notice

There is an exception to the rule that you start with a Statement of Claim. If your application is for construction (clarification) of a will only, then you would use an Originating Notice instead of a Statement of Claim. Clarification or construction of a will means that you are asking the court to interpret words or phrases in the will that are unclear or unfinished. (See the download kit included with this book for an example.)

You do not use a Statement of Claim for a clarification of will lawsuit because you aren't actually suing anyone. If you are the executor of the estate, you are neutral on the subject. You don't advocate for or against the meaning of words or phrases; you ask the court neutrally what it thinks. You are asking the court for an interpretation or assistance and not to pick sides between anyone. Therefore it wouldn't be appropriate to call anyone a defendant.

2. Interlocutory Applications

It is important to understand the difference between a Statement of Claim and interlocutory documents. You would only start your lawsuit once, so there is only one Statement of Claim. By contrast, there may be one or several interlocutory matters all on the same file and all happening after you begin your lawsuit.

For example, let's say that you file a Statement of Claim alleging that the testator did not have full knowledge and approval of his will. By doing that, you've started matters rolling and the end goal is either a settlement or a trial. Before you get to settlement or trial, there could be a number of interlocutory or interim applications you must deal with. Some will be brought by you and some by the opposing people. Some of them might be —

- to strike out some of your opponent's documents,

- to dismiss the other side's claim as having no merit (summary judgment),

- to serve documents on someone outside the province,

- to ask for costs,

- to ask the court for help when the parties cannot agree on what should happen next, or

- to set a date for a trial.

It would be impossible to list all of the potential applications because lawsuits vary so much. Hopefully this list will help you see that anything that is interlocutory is a preliminary step and not the final trial of the main issue.

Interlocutory applications can be either ex parte or inter partes. Most of the time, your applications will be inter partes, which translates as "between parties." That simply means that there is someone opposing you or expected to oppose you, and that person is given notice of your application. It is very rare that you would bring an application that is ex parte, or "in the absence of any other parties." If you bring an ex parte application that should be inter partes, the court will direct you to give notice to the defendant and come back on another day.

You will note that once the lawsuit has been started, either you or the people on the opposing side can start one of these interlocutory applications. When that happens, the person who starts the application is then called the applicant and the person who is on the other side is called the respondent. This changing of names can be confusing. You could be the plaintiff and the applicant, or you could be the plaintiff and the respondent. Then on the next application it could be the other way around. It all depends on who brings any given interlocutory application.

3. Filing a Caveat

It is useful to determine at which point the estate stands when you begin your lawsuit. Your options are:

1. The will has not yet been sent to the court for probate or there is no will.

2. The will is currently at the court waiting for probate to be granted by the judge or there is an application pending for someone to be given Letters of Administration.

3. The court has already granted Letters of Probate or Letters of Administration.

If you don't know whether the will has been sent to the court for probate and the executor won't provide that information, you should go to the courthouse nearest where the deceased lived to do a search. You will search on the name of the deceased to see whether anything has been filed. The clerks of the court will assist you with that. Make sure you have the right name of the deceased and the approximate date of death. There is a very small fee for the search (in most places, about $25). A few jurisdictions in Canada offer online searches but in most places you will have to go in person to the courthouse.

If nothing has yet been filed, or if the will is at the court but not yet probated, you should start by filing a caveat. A caveat is a brief document that alerts the court to the fact that someone has a problem with the estate and that person intends to request a hearing in court. Do not file a caveat if you are not serious about challenging the estate. The download accompanying this book contains a form of caveat for each province and territory with the exception of Nova Scotia, which does not allow caveats against estates. In British Columbia, a caveat against an estate is called a Notice of Dispute. In Ontario, it is called a Notice of Objection.

Once you file your caveat, the person who is applying to the court to probate the will or to obtain Letters of Administration cannot proceed until —

- your caveat has expired,

- you withdraw your caveat, or

- the issue has been dealt with by a judge.

Usually the procedure is that you file the caveat, then the parties who are trying to probate the will require you to show up in court and explain why you have filed the caveat. At that point, the judge will give some directions to the parties as to what to do next. You are likely to be directed to file your lawsuit within a certain amount of time, and that is when you will file the Statement of Claim as outlined in this chapter.

Table 4 shows how long your caveat or notice lasts before it expires. You may renew a caveat if you take steps to renew it before the expiry date. If you let the time expire, you cannot renew it without the court's permission.

The form of the caveat varies greatly from one province to the next, but one thing that every form has in common is a requirement

TABLE 4
CAVEAT EXPIRY TIMES

Province or Territory	Time before Caveat or Notice Expires
Alberta	3 months
British Columbia	1 year
Manitoba	12 months
New Brunswick	6 months
Newfoundland and Labrador	1 year
Northwest Territories	3 months
Nova Scotia	N/A
Nunavut	3 months
Ontario	3 years
Prince Edward Island	3 months
Saskatchewan	3 months
Yukon	6 months

that you provide an address for service. This means an address to which legal documents and correspondence may be sent to you. You may use your home address or a post office box. This address must be within the province or territory in which you are filing the caveat. You will note that in some cases, the forms require you to provide a second means of contacting you other than by mail, such as by email or fax.

Note that filing a caveat is not mandatory. It is a useful tool and possibly the simplest and best way to start your lawsuit but you can skip filing the caveat and go straight to the Statement of Claim if you wish.

4. What Forms Do I Need?

To start your lawsuit, you need to prepare the following documents:

1. **Statement of Claim:** This document initiates the lawsuit, announces who is suing whom, and identifies what the lawsuit is about. (Alternatively, the Originating Notice.)

2. **Affidavit supporting your claim:** This document contains the affidavit evidence of the parties to the lawsuit, from the basics such as the name of the deceased person to the details that describe exactly what happened to cause the lawsuit. You must file at least one affidavit. You may file more than one if there are multiple plaintiffs.

3. **Notice:** This document advises the defendant that he or she is being sued and gives him or her a deadline as to when to respond.

4. **Affidavit of service:** This document proves to the court that you gave the proper documents to the right people at the right time.

Note that in some jurisdictions, some of these documents on the list are combined so that the Notice is already part of the Statement of Claim. In the forms that go with this book, I have amalgamated the Notice and the Statement of Claim in those jurisdictions so that you do not have to prepare two separate documents. There are also variations on the name of the Notice between jurisdictions. Make sure you use the checklist for your province to ensure that you have the right forms.

5. Where Exactly Do I Start My Lawsuit?

In each province or territory, you will sue in the superior (higher) court, which has different names in different parts of the country. Table 5 shows the name of the superior court in your province or territory.

In almost every circumstance you should start the lawsuit in the province or territory in which the deceased person normally lived (note that where the person died could be different from where he or she lived). If there has already been an action started for Letters Probate or Letters of Administration, that is the province in which you must begin your lawsuit. The provinces are divided internally into separate geographical areas called judicial districts or judicial centers. Again, you should begin your lawsuit in the judicial district in which the deceased lived. This is easy to do if the deceased lived in a city or town that has a courthouse. Just by going to that nearby courthouse you would be sure of filing in the right place. If the person lived rurally and you are not sure which district is the right one, ask the Clerk of the Court at any courthouse in the correct province before you file your paperwork.

Table 5 also lists the fee that you will have to pay to the Clerk of the Court when you file your Statement of Claim.

Note that these are not the only fees you will have to pay during your lawsuit. These are the fees for filing your first document and starting your claim, but there will be other, smaller items along the way. In some cases you will be required to pay an additional fee

for further steps in court such as setting a trial date or obtaining a court order. In other cases you might need to certify documents or get photocopies from the court, all of which will cost extra.

If you are working with a lawyer, you should expect the lawyer to pay these smaller items on your behalf along the way. The lawyer will then either bill you for them in due course, or take them out of the retainer you provided in advance. If you are working on your own case without a lawyer, make sure you keep every receipt for every expense, clearly labelled as to its purpose, and dated. If you are successful in your lawsuit, you may well be able to claim these expenses back from the person you are suing.

6. How Do I Serve Documents on Someone?

Serving a document on someone means giving him or her a copy of it in the right way and at the right time. The point of serving the person is to ensure that he or she has been given proper notice of the court proceedings. This means giving the person the documents we have discussed in this chapter that set out your lawsuit and what it's all about so he or she knows what is going on. It also means giving the notice in time for him or her to defend against your lawsuit. The judge will always enforce the rules about service of documents in the interest of fairness to all parties. If you find that you cannot serve the defendant because he or she lives in another province or country, or you cannot find a fixed address, you may ask the judge for guidance and permission to use some other method of service.

You should always serve photocopies (and not originals) of the documents on the other parties. Most original documents will be kept by the court, but you should keep any

TABLE 5
WHERE TO FILE YOUR STATEMENT OF CLAIM

Province or Territory	Name of the Appropriate Court	Cost of Filing a Statement of Claim or Originating Notice
Alberta	Court of Queen's Bench of Alberta	$250
British Columbia	Supreme Court of British Columbia	$208
Manitoba	Court of Queen's Bench of Manitoba	$225
New Brunswick	Court of Queen's Bench of New Brunswick	$100
Newfoundland and Labrador	Supreme Court of Newfoundland and Labrador	$120
Northwest Territories	Supreme Court of the Northwest Territories	$165
Nova Scotia	Supreme Court of Nova Scotia	$211
Nunavut	Nunavut Court of Justice	$200
Ontario	Superior Court of Justice	$220
Prince Edward Island	Supreme Court of Prince Edward Island	$100
Saskatchewan	Court of Queen's Bench of Saskatchewan	$200
Yukon	Supreme Court of Yukon	$140

original documents that come into your possession and are not required by the court. The documents you must serve are the following:

1. Statement of Claim

2. Affidavit in support of your claim, with all exhibits attached

3. Notice to Defendant

There are different methods of service that you may wish to use in the next sections.

6.1 Personal service by you

Personal service of documents means giving the documents to the person you are suing and telling the person that these are legal documents. You can give them anywhere, such as the person's home, yard, or place of business. Of course, some people are not particularly happy to be served with legal documents, so it does not always go as smoothly as you might hope.

Don't be dismayed if the person you're suing refuses to accept the documents from you. His or her refusal will not stop you from having proper service, though the person might hope that to be the case. If it were that easy to avoid service, no lawsuit would have a chance of going ahead! If the person will not accept the documents, simply say that these are important legal papers and leave them where the person will have access to them after you have left. If you are in the person's home, shop, or office, simply leave the documents lying on a table or counter in plain sight. If you are outdoors, you could leave the documents in the mailbox, between the front doors, or rolled up behind the doorknob.

If the person you are suing is not at home, you may leave the documents with anyone who lives in the house who appears to be an adult.

Make careful note of the date, time, place, and method of service of the documents so that you may prepare an affidavit of service, which will be discussed in this chapter.

6.2 Personal service by a process server

This method also involves the documents being dropped off or given to the person you are suing, but not by you. A process server is a person whose job it is it to deliver documents in cases just like yours. This might be a good choice for you if you would find it dangerous, uncomfortable, or unpleasant to approach the defending person directly. It can also be a good choice if you are simply too busy to handle it yourself or you live too far away.

A process server will deliver the documents to the person and address that you supply to him or her, then report back to you on the details of the service, such as whether the person accepted the documents or they were left in the mailbox. Process servers are familiar with affidavits of service and will sign one for you to prove that they served the documents. A process server will usually bill you a flat rate for the service itself plus a charge per kilometre that he or she had to drive to serve the documents.

6.3 Registered mail

You may serve someone by writing him or her a letter saying he or she is being served and enclosing the necessary documents, and sending the package by registered mail. Ask for the type of mailing in which the party who receives the package must sign for it. That way you will have the information you need for your affidavit of service. You can track registered mail and see the signature online. Keep the receipt that the post office gives you because you will attach it to your Affidavit of Service to prove when you sent it.

6.4 Sending it to the other party's lawyer

If you know for sure that the person you are suing has a lawyer who is dealing with the estate matter, you should serve the documents on that lawyer. Whenever a person is represented by a lawyer, you should contact the lawyer first. If the lawyer tells you that he or she is not involved in it, then you can serve the documents directly on the person you're suing. If you're not sure whether the person has a lawyer, you would be better off serving on the person himself or herself.

When serving documents on someone's lawyer, you may drop off the documents at the lawyer's office, have someone else drop them off for you, or mail them. As with other methods of service, you will prepare an Affidavit of Service.

6.5 Time limits for service

There are time limits for when you must serve the documents. All of the time limits are linked to the court date you have set. Each time limit tells how many days before the court date the other person must receive the documents. For example, serving a document with two clear days means that you serve it with at least two full business days between the day you serve it and the court date. You can give more notice if you wish, but you cannot give less.

If you give less notice than what is required by the Rules of Court, the people opposing your lawsuit may simply ask the judge for more time to prepare to defend themselves. Most likely they would be successful in this request. If you don't give the proper amount of service and nobody shows up in court to oppose your application, the court may adjourn your hearing against your wishes until you can prove that you have given proper notice.

In Table 6, you will see the time limits that apply to your lawsuit or your application. As mentioned, these are the minimum acceptable deadlines. It is better to serve your documents a few days early than to risk missing the deadline and having everything delayed.

You will note that if you are the person starting the lawsuit, the opposing party does not have to give you ten days' notice. You are required to do that for them because you are the one setting the date and setting the agenda and therefore you already know what the matter is all about; they only have to respond. They must serve their affidavit on you within two clear days of the court date on an originating document, and one clear day on an interlocutory application. If they respond with information you didn't know before and you are taken by surprise, this time period may seem too short. However, that is the allowable time and you will have to either accept it or ask the court for an adjournment to allow yourself more time to absorb and deal with their defense.

If you are suing more than one person, you must serve each of them separately. The exception to this rule is that if you know that two or more of the defendants already have a lawyer handling the estate, you may serve that lawyer on behalf of all of the people who are working with that lawyer.

7. Affidavit of Service

As mentioned in this chapter, there are court rules that require you to give certain documents to the person or people you are suing. There are also rules about how and when to serve them. In order for you to prove to the court that your lawsuit was commenced properly and fairly, you will prepare an Affidavit of Service and file it at the court.

An affidavit is a document that you swear in front of a Commissioner for Oaths or a Notary Public. When you swear it, this has the same legal effect as if you swore it in court. In the affidavit of service you will describe —

TABLE 6
TIME LIMITS FOR SERVICE

The Documents You Are Serving	Time Limit for Service
Your originating document (e.g., Statement of Claim) and the affidavit(s) supporting your originating document	10 clear days
Notice of your Interlocutory Application and the affidavit(s) supporting your application	2 clear days
Any document being served on someone outside of your province	Minimum of 30 clear days unless a judge orders otherwise
Your supplementary affidavit on your originating document	3 clear days
Your supplementary affidavit on your interlocutory application	1 clear day

CHECKLIST 3
BEGINNING YOUR LAWSUIT

1. [　] Serve the documents on the defendants.

2. [　] Gather any proof such as postal receipts.

3. [　] Prepare the affidavit of service and attach the exhibits.

4. [　] Swear the affidavit in front of a Commissioner for Oaths or Notary Public.

5. [　] File the signed, sworn affidavit at the court where you started your action.

6. [　] Take the filed affidavit with you to court on the first day in case the judge asks to see it.

- which documents you served,

- who served the documents,

- how you served them (delivery, in person, registered mail, etc.),

- when you served them, and

- on whom you served them.

There are some additional exhibits that must be attached:

- A copy of each document you served.

- Any post office receipt for registered mail, signature on receipt, etc.

- Courier slip if served by courier.

If you use a process server or someone else to serve the documents instead of you, the affidavit will be completed and signed by that person rather than by you.

8. Court Dates

8.1 Court dates for trials

The process for obtaining court dates varies according to the type of matter being heard (i.e., trial versus interlocutory), jurisdiction, local practice, the time needed to conduct preliminary matters, and the length of time required to conduct the trial. In other words, it is impossible to describe a process that works for everyone in every case.

Trial dates are set by a trial coordinator. In smaller centers, the trial coordinator may be one clerk who works out of the local probate office. In larger centers, there may be a full staff of people working together as the local trial coordinators. In every case, the trial coordinator will consult the calendar to see when time is available and will give you the first available date that works for you and the opposing people. Sometimes it will be necessary to work around other commitments such as the lawyer on the other side already being booked for court on another matter on the same day. Do not be surprised if the trial date you are given is a year or more in the future.

By the time the trial date arrives, you are expected to have completed all paperwork, all cross-examinations on affidavits, and all of your preliminary (interlocutory) applications.

When you file your Statement of Claim, you will likely not be given a date of any kind to start with. Do not worry about that, as you are only in the first stages.

Once you have served your documents and the other side has responded, you can assess whether there is room for compromise or negotiation, or whether it needs to go forward through the courts. Remember that you have several steps to finish before getting a trial date.

When you have completed the appropriate tasks such as interlocutory applications and cross-examinations, you may go personally to the trial coordinator to discuss when your trial can take place. Be sure to take note of how much time is booked for the trial; it could be one day or it could be a week or more. The trial date might also be set by a judge in Chambers if you and the other party are there on an interlocutory application and the judge determines there is something that cannot be decided in any method other than a trial.

8.2 Court dates for interlocutory applications

Dates for interlocutory applications may be set in a variety of ways. The usual way is to take your application to the Clerk of the Court for filing, and for the clerk to provide you with the date at the same time. Depending on how full the court calendar is at any given time and how long you expect your application to take, you should expect to obtain a date anywhere from two days to two weeks out. You will have some say in which date is given, if there is a particular date that you are unavailable due to travel or other commitments.

It is not always easy to estimate how long your application will take, but this is information that the Clerks of the Court will request. They are trying to fit everyone into the available timeslots and to make the best use they can of every open courtroom. If you are simply going to set a date or ask for an adjournment, you can tell the clerk that you only need five minutes. If, on the other hand, you expect to proceed on an issue, tell the clerk that you will need time enough for the matter to be argued by both parties.

If the opposing party is the applicant on an interlocutory matter, they will file their own application and be given a court date. They will then serve documents on you and tell you about the date they have been given. You are expected to show up on that date even if it is inconvenient. If you do not show up, you risk losing on that issue and possibly on other matters (such as costs). If the date given to you by the other side is simply impossible for you, first let the applicant know and ask if they are willing to adjourn to another date. If they will not agree to that, you must show up in court or have someone show up on your behalf.

Another way that interlocutory dates are set is for a judge to order that your application is going to be heard on a certain day. This often happens in chambers when the judge sets a deadline, adjourns part of your application, or simply wants all of the parties to show up and give the court an update on what is happening. If you are in court and the judge wants to set a date, he or she will ask the Clerk of the Court in the courtroom for the next available date. You will be asked if that date works for you.

If at any time you are not sure of how to get a hearing date, ask the Clerk of the Court what to do. The clerk is allowed to give you this information and can be generally very helpful when non-lawyers ask for assistance.

9
Proving Your Case

In the descriptions of grounds for contesting a will and for chambers applications, I have listed the elements of the lawsuit. In every case, you must prove those elements in order to win your case. You cannot win with only some of the elements; all of them are essential and must be proved.

1. What Is the Standard of Proof?

Over the years, I have met many earnest and well-meaning individuals who tell me that they are confident of a win in court because they are truthful and what they are doing is morally right. In some cases they are so sure of victory that they won't even consider settlement options. I find that blind faith in your own just deserts to be extremely naive. You cannot take anything for granted in a court of law.

Telling your story to the judge is not enough. Don't forget that the people opposing you are going to tell a story, too. Theirs will be a different story from yours and it is the truth in their eyes if not in yours. The fact that you believe your side to be the one that deserves to win is important but, again, it's not enough to believe that it's as easy as just asking the judge to believe you. The judge will be faced with two — or perhaps several — sides to the story and everyone will feel that his or her version is the one that should win. You need to prove it.

Throughout this chapter, we will discuss how to go about proving the various elements of each issue. The facts and allegations that you bring forward must meet what is called the standard of proof. This refers to how strong your proof must be and how much room there is for doubt. Those who watch courtroom dramas on television often hear the TV lawyers refer to proving their case beyond a reasonable doubt. That standard of proof applies to criminal charges against people, so that if the charges against someone are not proved beyond a reasonable doubt, the accused person will go free.

The standard for civil law, which includes estate litigation, is different. It is referred to as a balance of probabilities. This means the court has to believe that most likely the story you are telling is true. It is not as strict a standard as "beyond a reasonable doubt."

2. Who Has Burden of Proof?

Burden of proof refers to the idea that certain parties have a responsibility to prove the elements of their case. If the burden of proof is on you, it means that you are the one with the responsibility to prove your case and if you fail to do so, you lose your case. There is no simple catch-all rule that says who has the burden of proof in all cases; it shifts back and forth at different stages in the proceedings. In Chapters 2 through 5, there was discussion of the grounds for contesting wills that covers who must prove which elements to win the lawsuit.

3. Does It Matter If Probate Has Already Been Granted?

There is a widespread belief out there, even among lawyers, that you cannot contest the validity of a will (remember, this means attacking it on the grounds laid out in Chapter 2), if the court has already given the executor a grant of probate. However, that is simply not true. The thinking behind the misconception is that the court has already established the validity of the will so it must be too late to challenge it.

The mistake arises from a lack of understanding of how wills are processed by the probate court. Almost all wills in Canada that go to the probate court are put through what can only be described as an express lane process. It is known as an informal probate process. The court relies on the executor putting forward true information. There is no investigation into any issues because no issues have been raised. The grant of probate is based on the information provided. This works well almost all of the time, since most people are honest and most wills are valid.

If there are problems or issues such as the grounds for contesting that we have discussed in this book, then it is up to the person who knows about the issues to bring them to the attention of the court. If the court agrees that there is a valid issue that needs to be heard, then the chambers judge will take back ("revoke") the grant of probate. A date will be set for a full hearing of all the evidence dealing with the issue that has been raised so that the judge may decide whether or not the will is valid.

The fact that a grant of probate has been issued already does not stop a person's right to raise an issue. It would be very unfair for this to be any other way, since most people have no idea what is in someone else's will until that will is sent to the probate court. Here is an example:

Mary was the mother of four children. When Mary got older, she said many times that her kids would all be treated equally. That was how she treated them as children and as adults, making sure that everything was fair and equal among them all. She had a good relationship with each of them. When Mary was in her 80s, she became ill and spent the last two months of her life in the hospital. After Mary's death, her daughter Maureen told her siblings that she had Mary's will and that Mary had appointed her as the executor. Maureen put the will through the probate court and received a grant of probate. Maureen was reluctant to give copies of the will to anyone, and it was three months after the probate was granted that the other children managed to get a copy. Once they saw the will, they were shocked. The will left almost everything to Maureen, going against everything their mother had told them about her plans. They also noticed that the will had been signed only a week before Mary's death when they knew that Mary had been weakened and disoriented by heavy medication. As they looked into the situation further, Mary's children became convinced that Maureen had influenced their mother into making a new will in Maureen's favour. Maureen was already busy transferring all of her mother's assets to herself.

In a case like this where the other family members don't see the will until after it has been sent to probate, the family may still challenge the will. However, they would have to move quickly because the judge will demand an explanation of why they didn't act as soon as they found out about the situation. If the amount of time that has passed is unreasonable in the situation, the judge may decide that it's too late for them to make a claim. There is no deadline set down for this because every case is different. Anyone in this situation should waste no time bringing their lawsuit to court.

4. Whom Exactly Do I Have to Sue?

You must be extremely careful when setting up your lawsuit that you name the right person or people. If you make a mistake, you could lose your case on the technicality that you sued the wrong people.

Whenever you launch a lawsuit against an estate, you are actually suing the people who represent the estate. This means you must name the executors or administrators of the estate as defendants (or, in interlocutory applications, as respondents). If there are co-executors, name both or all of them, even if the matter you're suing about involves one more than it involves the others. Failing to name the executors will likely end your lawsuit before it even gets started. Do not sue the alternate executors unless they are now the ones in charge of the estate. The alternates are the people who are named in a will to take over if the original executors pass away or refuse the job.

In will challenges based on undue influence, there is also a case against the person that you believe unduly influenced the testator. This means you must name that person in his or her personal capacity even if you have already named them as defendant executors. For example, let's say that you are bringing a lawsuit based on undue influence because you believe that your brother, Sam Green, influenced your mother into making changes to her will. Sam also happens to be the executor. On your Statement of Claim, Sam would be named twice as a defendant, as follows:

BETWEEN:

JACK GREEN
PLAINTIFF

AND

SAM GREEN, EXECUTOR OF THE ESTATE OF MARY GREEN
DEFENDANT

AND

SAM GREEN IN HIS PERSONAL CAPACITY
DEFENDANT

---

5. What's a Frivolous or Vexatious Lawsuit?

This phrase refers to a lawsuit that has been launched primarily to embarrass, inconvenience, or harass someone. It probably comes as no surprise that some people like to use the court system as a hammer to try to beat down someone they don't like or who has done something that is adverse to what they want. It should also come as no surprise that the courts are aware of this and have a way to deal with it.

A frivolous or vexatious lawsuit usually has little or no merit. In some cases there may be a so-so case but the real reason for the case is that the plaintiff is being spiteful toward the defendant. Obviously the court does not want these cases to happen. The court will throw them out if the defendant is successful in showing that the suit is frivolous or vexatious. In addition to tossing out the case, the judge will generally punish the plaintiff who wasted everyone's time and money by ordering that the plaintiff pay the defendant's legal costs.

6. What Evidence Will I Need and How Do I Get It?

The evidence required in any lawsuit will of course depend on the facts of your case. In each of the grounds for challenging a will set out in this book, I have listed the elements of the grounds. If you are challenging a will, you must prove all of the elements. For example, the list of elements of undue influence includes these three items:

1. Someone influenced the testator in some way, such as threats, force, trickery, lies, persuasion, shaming, isolation, control over daily living, or persistent requests. It is likely to be a combination of more than one method.

2. The influence overpowered the testator's mental or emotional freedom so that the testator felt he or she had no choice but to go along with it.

3. The testator made a will that he or she would not have made without that influence.

This means that if you are alleging that undue influence was present in the will you are challenging, you must prove that ALL of these elements are present in your case. It is not enough to prove one or two. You can see how they all fit together. If you are defending against a challenge by someone alleging undue influence, you need only prove that any one of the essential elements is missing in order to defeat the application. Once you know which of the grounds you wish to rely on or what kind of application you want to bring, check the list of required elements above.

For each of the elements, you will ask yourself who has information that you can use to prove your case. Your own testimony — your telling of the facts — may of course be given and it will be valuable, but you absolutely must have independent, third-party information to back you up. There may be doubt cast on your testimony because you stand to gain from it. Testimony from the various parties involved in a lawsuit tends to be a "he said, she said" situation in which the judge has to choose who seems to be the most credible person. However, a third party will have nothing to gain from your lawsuit and is therefore considered to give stronger evidence.

Wherever possible, find paperwork or online records that you can use to prove each and every bit of what you are saying. This may add up to a lot of paperwork, but it is all important. Some paperwork is obviously valuable, such as doctors' reports, but also turn your mind to other, less obvious ways of backing up what you say. If you are alleging that your brother isolated your mother in order to influence her, get the records from the care facility that show all the times you showed up there but were not allowed to see your mother. If you're alleging that the executor gave the deceased's car to someone who was not entitled to receive it, take a picture of that person driving the car or parking it in his or her garage. Think about receipts, emails, text messages, photos, screenshots of a Facebook post, credit card bills, phone records — anything that independently backs up any fact of your story.

7. "Best Evidence" Guidelines

Any time you choose an item of evidence to support your case, you try to find the best and most persuasive evidence available on that issue. Remember that the point of all of the evidence you will bring during your lawsuit is to persuade the judge that the request you are making should be granted. The party on the other side of the courtroom will be doing everything he or she can to persuade the judge against you, so your evidence needs to be clear, strong, and wherever possible, backed up by something that was not produced by you. The opposing party will try to poke holes in your evidence. Though the court will likely allow you to introduce all evidence that it believes to be relevant to the case, you will want each and every piece of evidence to be the strongest version you are able to find.

There are guidelines for coming up with the best evidence that you can. They are:

1. An original is better than a photocopy.

2. Evidence written or taken at the time of an event is better than evidence that was reconstructed from memory after some time.

3. Independent evidence is better than self-serving evidence.

4. Recent or timely material is better than old or outdated material.

5. Only relevant material may be used.

The guidelines above mention that only relevant material may be used. This is where many people have a great deal of trouble staying on track. When you are involved in an emotional case, it can be next to impossible to leave out details that you find upsetting. It's not easy to ignore things that cause you pain. However, you are going to have to be absolutely ruthless when it comes to your evidence and that of other witnesses. Including 10 or 20 pages full of tearful stories of how rude the executor was to everyone at the last family gathering may seem relevant and important to you, and it may even satisfy you to tell the court what a terrible person he or she is, but does it actually prove any of the legal elements of your case?

When you include a lot of material that is emotionally laden and full of denouncements of the other people in the lawsuit, many unexpected and negative outcomes can occur. Sometimes the impact of the evidence is that it upsets and inflames everyone, turning your lawsuit into a brawl in which everyone tries to hurt everyone else. There is nothing more pointless or painful than that. Nothing will get resolved and you will have wasted time and money aggravating an already upsetting situation.

In other cases, some of the details that really aren't all that relevant somehow seem to take over and gain all of the attention. Your case will get bogged down on a question of whether your brother pushed you into puddles when you were children three times rather than four times, when what you really want is for him to be removed as executor. All you've done is given the other side ammunition to sidetrack your case, slow it down, and cause you additional frustration. It can be easy to get sidetracked if there is irrelevant information given as evidence. Leave out the parts you don't really need.

Another danger of including irrelevant material is that the lawyer acting for the other party may be able to persuade the judge that everything you've said — all of your evidence — is irrelevant. You may be portrayed as a person who has put together a case full of nonsense because you had no real evidence of value to give. If this happens, your case may be thrown out by way of summary judgment or your case may be portrayed as being frivolous or vexatious. If that happens, you will not even have a chance to argue your case.

As you go through your own evidence or that of other witnesses who support you, ask yourself on each and every sentence: What point of law or fact does this sentence prove? Always remember that talking about something is not the same as proving it. Stay focused.

8. Types of Evidence Commonly Used in Estate Litigation

In this section, we will look at some of the different kinds of documents that many estate litigants use. While each individual case is unique, there are certain themes that recur because of the nature of estate litigation and the relatively few grounds for contesting wills. There will always be discussion and disputes over topics such as mental capacity of the testator and the integrity of the executor because those recurring concepts are at the center of estate litigation.

8.1 Capacity assessments

Whenever incapacity, undue influence, or lack of knowledge of the will is alleged, a capacity assessment can make or break a case because it talks about the testator's mental ability. As you know from reading the lists of essential elements, this evidence goes right to the heart of your case. Sometimes assessments are specifically prepared for the court hearing, but in most cases they already exist for other purposes. For example, a capacity assessment is frequently done when a senior moves into a long-term care facility so that the caregivers may assess the level of care that is needed for that individual to be safe and comfortable. Since estate litigation involves an argument about someone who has already passed away, a report that is prepared specifically for the court hearing would have to be put together using existing records rather than new information.

If there is a capacity assessment already in existence and you have access to it, you are allowed to use it to support your case. It does not have to be something that was prepared for your use specifically. This applies to the people opposing your application as well. You should be aware that if a capacity assessment exists that harms your case, you may choose not to use it but the party opposing you will probably use it to support his or her case.

When it comes to capacity assessments, consider the following points when choosing your best evidence:

1. **Was the person who prepared the report a physician, psychologist, psychiatrist, nurse, or perhaps some other type of assessor?** How much

experience does he or she have with preparing this kind of report? Does he or she specialize in geriatric medicine? Does he or she work in a care facility? The better the qualifications of the assessor, the more you can rely on the report.

2. **How well did the assessor know the testator?** Was it done by someone who had seen the testator many times over a number of years, or someone who only met the testator on the day of testing? This might make a difference in how much weight the court gives the capacity assessment, especially if there are conflicting reports.

3. **How much input did specific members of the family have into the content of the report?** Capacity assessments always contain facts and opinions of the immediate family members of the person being assessed but it is not always balanced among several individuals. In your case, did the report rely heavily on the opinion of the person who is now using the report to obtain a judgment? Is the information in the report self-serving or one-sided?

4. **How specific is the capacity assessment in terms of what the testator could or could not do at the time?** Was the assessment prepared to answer a specific question at the time? Does the report go into detail about whether the incapacity was about living independently, loss of memory, or lack of ability to handle finances and legal matters? This is extremely important; there is no point trying to establish lack of ability to write a will if your report only says that the testator could not cook and clean for himself or herself.

5. **Was the capacity assessment undertaken at a time that was close to the event in question?** For example, if incapacity or lack of knowledge are being alleged, was the assessment done around the time the will was signed? If you have an assessment that states the testator was suffering from advanced dementia, it is much more relevant if that report was made a month after the will was signed rather than a year or two after the will was signed.

8.2 Medical reports

Medical reports are not the same as capacity assessments. The assessments are usually done by doctors who specialize in disease or disability of the mind. They are done for the specific purpose of determining mental capacity. Medical reports, on the other hand, may be prepared by emergency room physicians, family doctors, community health nurses, paramedics, or even coroners. They are usually done for some other reason besides determining mental capacity but their contents may still be very revealing.

Medical reports contain information that may go to the heart of your case. If you are alleging that the testator did not have the ability to make a will, you may be able to support your case if there are reports that show the testator was taking heavy medication or was somehow ill. The report could back up your claim that the testator was not fully aware of what he or she was doing because of the influence of the medication.

For example, in a case of undue influence, there could be a medical report showing that the testator was admitted to a hospital in the recent past. If the report showed that the testator was at the time malnourished, dirty, and in generally poor condition, it may be concluded that the testator was vulnerable and dependent on others, or that he or she was being mistreated by caregivers.

When determining whether a specific medical report supports your case and follows the best evidence guidelines, the questions are much the same as they were regarding the capacity assessments. Who made the medical report? What are that person's qualifications? Is the person preparing the report neutral? How well did he or she know the testator? Was the patient seen many times or just once? How thorough is the report? Were the facts checked for accuracy before being included in the report? Were there mistakes made (such as not knowing what medications the patient was taking)?

8.3 Police reports

Most estate litigation does not involve police reports, but these reports can certainly be relevant when your lawsuit is about undue influence or mental capacity. If the police had any involvement with the testator, it could have an impact on your case. Here are some examples where it could affect things:

1. You are trying to prove that the testator's alcoholism was so severe that he or she was out of control and severely ill at the time the will was made. There may be a police report regarding impaired driving around that time.

2. You are trying to prove undue influence by the opposing party over the testator. There may be a police report where a neighbour reported witnessing physical abuse of the testator.

3. You may be trying to prove that the will was forged by a certain person. There may be a police report that this person had been convicted of fraud before.

Just be sure when you are using a police report that it does actually help to prove your point. If the report shows your opponent in a bad light but has nothing whatsoever to do with the case, you might feel as though you want to include it anyway to show that your opponent is a bad person. Resist that temptation and remember that the first rule of evidence is relevancy. Slinging mud at people for no good reason does not achieve your goals and as mentioned earlier, it may bounce back on you in detrimental ways.

8.4 Lawyer's file

Whenever a will is called into question, it is a good idea to get a copy of the notes and other materials in the file of the lawyer who prepared the will. These notes can clear up a lot of questions, though of course they may raise more questions as well.

When a lawyer meets a client to prepare a will, the lawyer should take notes about the client's goals and wishes. This can go a long way toward explaining a will in which someone was left out, or in which the lion's share of the estate was given to one person. If the lawyer is doing his or her job properly, he or she will ask questions when a client wants to do something unusual in a will. For example, if the client says that he or she wants to leave out one of the children, the lawyer should ask why the client wants to do that and make notes in the file about the client's answer. Sometimes you will find information about family relationships that has never been discussed or even known in the family before. Not all lawyers make detailed or extensive notes, but it is always worth getting the file to see what help it can offer.

If the client is elderly or in the hospital at the time of instructing the lawyer to make a will, the lawyer will often include notes about how the lawyer assessed the client's mental capacity. You will find that judges are very interested in this portion of the lawyer's file because it allows the judge to know exactly what the client was asked and exactly what answer was given.

Obtaining the lawyer's file might also be extremely useful if you are an executor applying to the court for clarification of words or phrases in the will. The lawyer might have taken notes about the testator's intentions that will help the court understand the testator's goals and wishes.

Acquiring the lawyer's file is not always easy. As you may know, lawyers owe a duty of confidentiality to their clients and as a result they may not discuss a client's business with anyone else. This duty extends to the client even after the client has passed away. Because of this, you may find that the lawyer will not simply hand over the file to you. If that is the case, you will have to call the lawyer as a witness at the trial (or at discovery/examination) to give answers directly in court.

8.5 Estate documents

In any will challenge, it is useful to see what other estate documents exist. Previous wills made by the testator can be extremely important. Let's say you are alleging that someone influenced the testator to change the will to give most of the estate to one of the testator's children. If you can show that over the last 40 years the testator made previous wills that all consistently gave the estate equally to all the children, you have definitely strengthened your case.

In addition, there are documents that, strictly speaking, are not estate documents but they are part of the testator's estate plan. They provide plenty of information about how the testator wanted his or her property distributed. This includes:

1. Title to property showing joint ownership

2. Statements showing joint ownership of bank accounts or investments

3. Life insurance policies naming a specific beneficiary

4. RRSPs or RRIFs naming a specific beneficiary

5. Trusts set up for beneficiaries

6. Prenuptial or cohabitation agreements

If you cannot obtain some of these items but you believe they would help your case, consider holding a cross-examination of a witness who could provide the information and asking the witness to undertake to give you the documents. Chapter 12 goes into detail about how and when to hold a cross-examination.

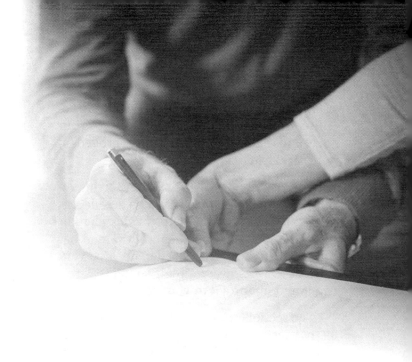

10
Preparing Affidavits

As discussed earlier in this book, many of your lawsuits will take place either partially or entirely in chambers. All of the evidence given by all of the witnesses in chambers is given in the form of a written, sworn statement called an affidavit. This means that nobody gives evidence orally in chambers and nobody is cross-examined in chambers. When someone is represented by a lawyer, only the lawyer speaks in chambers. If you are representing yourself, obviously you will speak for yourself, but your evidence must still be given in the form of an affidavit. The rules about this are very strict. If someone from the other side of the lawsuit objects to something you say in court on the basis that it is not in your affidavit, the judge will probably decide that you cannot say it. Because of this, it's very important for you to understand what goes into an affidavit and what form it should take. The following sections of this book will help you prepare the affidavit you need.

1. Different Kinds of Affidavits

During the course of your litigation, you are likely to prepare more than one affidavit. Some will be long and complicated and others will not. This is because the word "affidavit" represents a type of document that can be varied so that it is used for many purposes and in many situations. Your circumstances will determine which you will need. The following list discusses the various types of affidavits most often used in estate litigation.

1.1 Affidavit in support

No matter what kind of issue you bring to chambers, you will need an affidavit in support. There is no way around the fact that you are going to need to prepare at least one of these. This refers to an affidavit that contains evidence that proves the Statement of Claim or proves other matters. It is prepared specifically for the purpose of supporting your claims or requests. It is often very lengthy because, as mentioned earlier, every bit of your story must be written down and proved in your affidavit.

You usually only get one shot at this affidavit, so make it as clear and as detailed as you can. There are tips later in this chapter for preparing your document, but remember that it is alright for this document to be very thick as long as everything it contains is relevant and important to your case.

See section 1.5 about affidavits of service, as that section will tell you more about what to do with the Affidavit in Support once you have prepared it.

1.2 Affidavit in response

If you are the person suing the estate, an Affidavit in Response is not an affidavit you will prepare. Once you have given the defendant notice of your lawsuit, he or she will review your evidence and prepare an affidavit of his or her own, known as an Affidavit in Response. If there is more than one defendant, they may file one Affidavit in Response between them or they may choose to file one for each of them.

Make sure you read their evidence carefully so that you can decide whether you need to give more evidence of your own. Be prepared for the impact of reading the Affidavit in Response; most individuals find it very difficult to deal with the negative allegations against them that are put forward by relatives and friends. Many are angered by what they believe are lies or smears and are also very sad about the tattered state of the family structure. Before making any kind of reply to the Affidavit in Response, take the time to cool off. Once the initial affidavits are filed there is no set time limit for filing supplementaries.

Upon reading the Affidavit in Response, analyze its contents. It should contain the defendant's side of the story and may have third-party supporting evidence as well. As you read through it, try to pinpoint the places (if any) in which you and the defendant agree on what happened. There is no need to present argument to the judge on points that nobody is contesting so you can put those aside. Then take note of the parts of the affidavit which directly contradict your evidence given in your affidavit. Try to determine how strong the defendant's case is compared to yours. Does he or she make any good points? If so, what can you say or do to strengthen your case on those points?

The Affidavit in Response may also be accompanied by a Memorandum of Law and Argument. If the chambers application is for something brief such as setting a court date, there probably will not be a Memorandum filed by anyone as yet. However, as your lawsuit progresses and you go to chambers for more complicated matters, a Memorandum of Law and Argument is prepared to show how the facts in your affidavit prove the law is in your favour. There will be more information in Chapter 11 about how to deal with a Memorandum of Law and Argument.

1.3 Supplementary affidavit

You are not required to file a Supplementary Affidavit but you may do so if it helps your case. You do not get to keep filing more and more supplementary affidavits; you should only file one except in rare circumstances. The purpose of this type of affidavit is to address any new issues or unexpected developments that were raised in the Affidavit in Response. You also have the chance to add additional facts that perhaps you left out of your Affidavit in Support because you did not believe they were relevant until the matter was raised by the defendant.

These three kinds of affidavits discussed to this point (Affidavit in Support, Affidavit in Response, Supplementary Affidavit) are standard in estate litigation. Though every situation is unique, there is still an accepted structure for the court process. Here are the usual steps:

1. The plaintiff files a Statement of Claim and at the same time, an Affidavit in Support.

2. The plaintiff serves these two documents on the defendant.

3. The plaintiff files an Affidavit of Service proving he or she served the defendant.

4. The defendant files an Affidavit in Response.

5. The defendant serves the Affidavit in Response on the plaintiff.

6. If the Affidavit in Response brings up new issues or there is something important that must be said in rebuttal, the plaintiff may file a Supplementary Affidavit addressing those matters.

7. The plaintiff serves the Supplementary Affidavit on the defendant. (The rules contemplate each party filing one supplementary but generally do not forbid further affidavits. However, the judge may become irritated if you keep handing in more materials every time you think of a good comeback. The advice I give my client is that we get one supplementary only.)

8. Everyone appears in chambers to tell the judge what is happening, to deal with preliminary matters, and to set a date for a hearing.

1.4 Affidavit of execution

The Affidavit of Execution is an affidavit that states how and when a document was signed and/or witnessed. The affidavit is sworn by a witness who saw someone sign a document and can attest to the identity, age, and in some cases the mental capacity of the person who signed. The purpose of an Affidavit of Execution is to prove that all of the necessary formalities of signing a document were properly followed. It can be used on any kind of document and in many cases the court requires an Affidavit of Execution on certain documents.

The basics of an Affidavit of Execution are that it —

1. identifies the person who signed the document,

2. identifies the witness who saw the signing,

3. states that the witness was present at the relevant time to see the signing,

4. identifies the document that was signed, and

5. states the date on which the document was signed.

In addition, an Affidavit of Execution will confirm information that is specific to the first document that was signed. The purpose is to show that signing formalities were properly carried out. For example, a witness to the signing of a will cannot be a beneficiary of the will or the spouse of a beneficiary of the will. The Affidavit of Execution signed by the witness would state that he or she was not a beneficiary or spouse of a beneficiary in order to show that the signing was done in accordance with the legal rules. This is the part of the Affidavit of Execution that changes from document to document. In the context of wills, an Affidavit of Execution contains a statement that the witness believes the testator was mentally competent on the day the will was signed. In addition, the Affidavit of Execution addresses any unusual circumstances regarding the signing of a document, such as the person signing the document —

1. was blind and so the document was read to him or her in full before signing;

2. was ill or injured and couldn't sign his or her name and so signed with an "x"; or

3. doesn't speak the language in which the document is written and so a translator read and translated the will for him or her.

1.5 Affidavit of service

An Affidavit of Service serves a specific purpose. It is used to show the court that you served the opposing party with information about the lawsuit so that he or she could respond. If the opposing party or his or her lawyer shows up in court, the judge is unlikely to waste time asking you about service of the documents; the fact that the other people have shown up at the right time in the right place is all the evidence you need that they were given notice. However, if you attend court and the other party is not there, it will be up to you to prove you gave them proper notice. The judge will not let your lawsuit go ahead if you cannot prove the defendant knows about it. Your Affidavit of Service is your proof.

Do not wait for your court date before preparing this affidavit. Prepare it as soon as you have served the documents and file it promptly at the courthouse. That way if proof of service is needed by the judge, you already have it at hand and the court already has a record.

2. Who Can Make an Affidavit?

In many cases, the only person giving an affidavit is the plaintiff himself or herself, so if you are the person applying to the court, yours may be the only affidavit given. Yours is not optional. However, you can get evidence from anyone who has something relevant to say about your lawsuit by having them sign and swear an affidavit as well. You will prepare one for yourself, but many chambers applications have several affidavits. Sometimes you have to get different people to tell parts of a story so that it adds up to a coherent full narrative. An affidavit contains evidence so it is to your advantage to get affidavits from anyone and everyone who has information that helps your case.

Let's say that you are bringing a lawsuit on the basis that the testator, your grandmother, did not have the mental capacity to make a will. Some of the people who might provide you with affidavit evidence are —

- the doctor who assessed your grandmother's mental capacity;

- the caregivers who came in to help your grandmother with daily tasks;

- the bankers your grandmother dealt with, particularly one who might have reached out to the family because of your grandmother's problems at the bank;

- family members who can testify about how your grandmother doesn't recognize them anymore or has other memory loss issues; or

- the lawyer she consulted to have her will prepared.

You can see how all of these people mentioned above have a different perspective on the same situation. Each has seen or heard something that the others have not and that the others cannot testify about. This is why getting an affidavit from each of them might be a good idea, so that the whole story is told.

Remember that the person who gives the information that goes into an affidavit must have firsthand knowledge of that information. The person has to swear that every word of it is true.

3. How Do I Write an Affidavit?

You need to know how to write, sign, and attach exhibits to your affidavit. Try the following technique for putting together your affidavit:

1. Write down (or type) your main points in any order they occur to you. Don't worry about spelling or punctuation or anything like that just yet. Just scribble down the points first.

2. Once you have the basic points down, go back and put them in the order in which they happened.

3. Then fill in more detail such as names, dates, and places.

4. Then add the conclusions you want the judge to reach when he or she reads your affidavit. For example, if you have described several instances in which your grandmother demonstrated lack of capacity, say so. State that the effect of all of these instances means your grandmother lacked the ability to make a will. Draw a direct line between your evidence and the judgment you want by showing how your evidence leads to that conclusion.

At this point, you have produced the first draft of your affidavit, but you are not finished yet. Once that is in place, go through the following sections in this chapter to ensure that your draft meets the requirements.

3.1 First person narrative

Your affidavit should be written in the first person so that it sounds like you telling your own story. In other words, if you are describing a conversation you had with the testator, you would say, "My grandmother told me that … " Only one person should tell the story in any given document. Each person gets his or her own affidavit.

3.2 Firsthand/personal knowledge

You can only give testimony about something you know firsthand. You cannot swear to something if you are only guessing it's true. Speculation is not truth. You can't say what happened at a certain event if you were not there, nor can you swear that something you heard from someone else is true, since your knowledge is secondhand and therefore it is hearsay.

Here is an example of something I hear frequently from beneficiaries in situations where they are concerned about estate finances:

"The executor won't give any financial information and I think he's hiding something. Now his son has a brand new, expensive car. He bought that car for his son out of the estate, I just know it."

If you are sitting around your dinner table with your family, making this sort of statement is your choice. However, it is not your choice to say something like that in an affidavit. You cannot swear that the executor bought the car, and you especially don't know whether estate funds were used to purchase it. It is alright to say you believe the executor is hiding something, since your belief is backed up by facts of which you have personal knowledge — your requests for information and the executor's refusal to respond to you. Keep in mind that your affidavit is court evidence. Swearing under oath to false evidence is perjury.

Start your affidavit with a statement of who you are with respect to the lawsuit, followed by a statement that you have firsthand, personal knowledge of everything you are about to say. For example, you might say:

I, JANE BEGONIA, am the daughter of the deceased and therefore have personal knowledge of the matters herein deposed to except where stated to be on information and belief.

You will note that the sentence about firsthand knowledge has an addition to it. You are allowed to include certain matters that were told to you. For example, let's say that your mother's doctor told you that she had major bruising that the doctor suspected came from physical abuse. You do not have personal knowledge of whether it came from physical abuse and to state as truth what you only know from the doctor is hearsay. However you DO have personal knowledge of the words the doctor said to you. Therefore you must be careful to say that you believe it was physical abuse because the doctor said so.

You could say:

I am advised by Dr. Rangoon and do believe that the bruises on my mother's body were likely caused by physical abuse.

You could NOT say:

The bruises on my mother's body were caused by physical abuse.

If you are going to include a statement that you believe something you were told, make sure you say who told you. Include a positive statement that you believe it, such as set out in the example above in which you believe what the doctor told you about the bruises.

3.3 Chronological order

Tell your story in chronological order. This will help keep you organized and help ensure that you don't miss anything important. It will certainly be much easier for the judge and other parties to read and understand your story as well.

3.4 Relevancy

It doesn't matter if your affidavit is lengthy, as long as everything in it is relevant to the lawsuit. You know something is relevant if it is directly related to the point of law you are relying on, or it directly shows a fact that is essential to the story. For example, in a lawsuit in which you are asking to remove an executor, it is relevant to list each and every time you asked for or demanded information about the estate assets without getting an answer. It is not relevant to say that when you were teenagers, the executor would never lend you his leather jacket.

You must stay on course and leave out things that bother you but simply do not have anything to do with the lawsuit. When I ask clients to write out their stories for me, I usually find that they contain quite a few emotion-laden anecdotes. There are often a lot of generalizations about other people's personalities and actions. Go back over the first draft of your affidavit and edit it mercilessly — take out anything that does not prove a point.

To help you decide what is relevant, go back to the chapters of this book that lists the elements of the law you are relying on (set out in Chapters 2 through 5). Ask yourself how each paragraph of your affidavit helps to prove one of the elements.

3.5 Paragraphs

Once you have included your introductory lines about who you are and your firsthand knowledge, you will tell your story and give your evidence. Make sure that you break the information down into many short paragraphs. If possible, give each idea or event its own paragraph, even if that paragraph ends up being only a line or two. It is simply much harder to read a document that is crowded and mashed together with no white space around it. You are trying to be persuasive, clear, and articulate, and formatting your document properly will help convey that impression.

Your paragraphs must be numbered, and so should your pages. You may use headings if your affidavit is very long and you are covering several major topics. For example, if you are making an affidavit to support your lawsuit that is addressing both resulting trust and unjust enrichment, you might wish to use headings to divide your affidavit between those two topics. Take a look at the sample affidavit in Sample 2 to see how your pages should look.

3.6 State the purpose

In the last or second to last paragraph of your Affidavit in Support or your Supplementary Affidavit, include a brief statement as to why you have made your affidavit. For example, you might say, "I make this affidavit in support of my request that the Executor be compelled to pass his accounts with the court." Keep it brief.

There is no need to include a statement of this kind in an Affidavit of Execution or an Affidavit of Service.

4. What Do I Do about Exhibits?

Throughout this book, we have talked about proving your case and not just telling your story. When you are giving evidence by way of affidavit, each individual piece of evidence that you use as back-up for your case is called an exhibit. You have to include each exhibit in your affidavit by marking it as explained below and attaching it in the right order. You will have your entire affidavit first, followed by the exhibits in order.

An exhibit will be either a document, a photograph, or an item such as a receipt or bank statement. The exhibits will vary depending on what you are trying to prove. If at all possible, use originals as discussed in Chapter 9, section 7. As an example, let's say that you are Joan Winter and you want to prove that the testator of a will did not have testamentary capacity when he signed his will. You have a medical report that confirms a diagnosis of dementia. In your affidavit you would say that you have this report and you would attach it as Exhibit "A." Your affidavit would say something like:

1. I, Joan Winter, believe that my father did not have testamentary capacity on the day he signed his will.

2. My belief that my father did not have testamentary capacity is supported by a report prepared by Dr. Sloane on July 10, 2018, that states my father lacked capacity to deal with legal documents. The original report prepared by Dr. Sloane is attached to this affidavit as Exhibit "A."

As you go through your affidavit, mention each exhibit that you are going to attach. They will all need to be attached together after the main body of your affidavit.

You must mark each exhibit with the letter that identifies it. Start at A and work your way through the alphabet. (If you actually make it to Z, start over at AA, BB, etc.) This means you must actually write on each of the exhibits. Write on the front of the first page of the exhibit if at all possible, even if you have to squeeze it in. If there simply is not enough room on the front of the first page, use the back of the first page. If your exhibit has more than one page, you only have to mark the first one. Using the example of Joan Winter above, Joan would write on the front of Dr. Sloane's report the following:

THIS IS EXHIBIT "A" IN THE AFFIDAVIT
OF JOAN WINTER

SWORN BEFORE ME AT THE CITY OF VANCOUVER,
PROVINCE OF BRITISH COLUMBIA,
THIS _____ DAY OF _____, 2018.

_____
A Commissioner for Oaths

---

5. Once It's Prepared, What Do I Do with It?

Once your supporting affidavit contains all of your evidence and you are satisfied that it is written as clearly as possible, you will sign and swear it in front of a Commissioner for Oaths. If you are swearing your affidavit for use in another province, make sure you swear it in front of a Notary Public instead of a Commissioner for Oaths. The Notary or Commissioner will sign the affidavit, stamp it with his or her stamp, and will sign and stamp each exhibit as well.

When that step is complete, make several copies of your affidavit and take them to the courthouse to be filed. Do this at the same time as filing your Statement of Claim.

After filing, you will serve copies of your documents on the various parties to the lawsuit. You will find more information and instructions about service of documents in Chapter 8.

SAMPLE 2
AFFIDAVIT IN SUPPORT

I, NORMAN BROWN, MAKE OATH AND SAY THAT:

1. I am the son of the deceased, ISABELLA BROWN, and a beneficiary under her will, and as such I have personal knowledge of the matters herein deposed to, except where stated to be based on information and belief.

2. My mother passed away on January 12, 2018, and Letters Probate were granted to my brother, WILTON BROWN, on March 28, 2018. Attached as Exhibit "A" to this affidavit is a copy of the Letters Probate.

3. WILTON BROWN has asked me to sign a release which approves of his accounting of the estate, but has not provided me with a proper accounting.

4. I received an accounting from WILTON BROWN, a copy of which is attached as Exhibit "B" to this affidavit in September of 2018 but this accounting is incomplete. There are funds in the amount of $35,000 unaccounted for. In addition, the expenses claimed by WILTON BROWN are excessive.

5. I have tried several times to obtain information from WILTON BROWN but he will not respond. Attached as Exhibit "C" to this affidavit are copies of eight (8) emails and letters I sent to WILTON BROWN requesting information about the missing funds. I have never received any response.

6. I make this affidavit in support of a request that this Honourable Court compel WILTON BROWN to pass his accounts in the estate of ISABELLA BROWN.

SWORN BEFORE ME at the City   )
of Winnipeg, in the Province of Manitoba   )
this 18th day of December, 2018.   )

_____
Signature of
NORMAN BROWN

_____
A Commissioner for Oaths

My commission expires _____

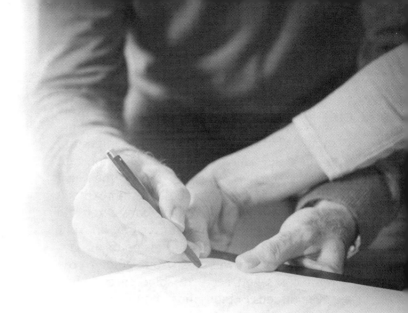

11

Preparing a Memorandum of Law and Argument

1. Legal Research to Support Your Case

Many people are familiar with provincial small claims court, in which a person can do very little preparation, then show up on the court day and simply tell his or her story. The judge applies the law to the case and makes a decision about the case based on the facts. Do not make the mistake of thinking that going to chambers is anything like small claims court. It is not enough just to tell your story.

If your case is going to court, you need to know the law that supports you. You will have to present your position to the judge and support it by showing how the law backs you up. The people who are opposing your lawsuit will also attempt to persuade the judge that the law favours them. If you are in the chambers level of court, which is basically everything except a full-blown trial, you will have to prepare and file a written Memorandum of Law and Argument (also called a brief or

a factum) that tells your story and describes the law that you are relying on. This means that you will have to do some legal research.

2. Secondary Sources

I strongly suggest that before you start looking up specific cases that support your case, find a secondary source and read about the topic that is covered by your case. A textbook is a secondary source, as are books like the one you are now reading, while the individual court cases themselves are primary sources. Secondary sources are prepared by researchers, lawyers, and others who have read the primary sources and have summarized where the law stands on various topics.

For example, if you are planning a lawsuit to try to remove an executor, find a textbook that talks about removal of executors. Read about why the law permitting removal of executors exists and what it is supposed to do. Read about which cases were successful and which were not, and find out why they were successful or not. What do they have in common? What did the judge say was important to the case? This step is extremely important because in the secondary source the legal concepts will be explained and the textbook will tell you which cases are considered the leading (or most important) cases on your topic. It will save you countless hours or days of research and will be a strong guide to the right cases you need. In some cases it will save you tens of thousands of dollars because it may explain to you that you are misunderstanding the law and that you should not be taking anyone to court.

Note that there are some secondary sources that are used by lawyers and judges within the wills and estates industry and you should use those too if you possibly can. They are considered reliable and accurate by the courts and are therefore accepted when you quote them or rely on them in your arguments. They are also updated on a regular basis so that new cases are added to the discussion. You can be confident that what you are reading is correct and up-to-date, and written by someone with true experience in the field. Do not under any circumstances rely on publicly written sources such as Wikipedia, as their purpose is for general information only and not for inclusion in legal briefs.

You must also be careful to ensure that you are not using sources that are from another country. There are a lot of American books, articles, and webpages containing quite a bit of legal material, but these will not be helpful to you. Any material from outside of Canada is not acceptable. The law is not the same everywhere and it is essential that you use only those that are applicable. You will find that in the best secondary sources, the authors will direct you to cases or principles that exist in each province.

The following are some of the best secondary sources on wills and estates matters:

- *Waters' Law of Trusts in Canada*, 4th edition (Carswell, 2012)

- *Oosterhoff on Trusts: Text, Commentary and Materials*, 8th edition (Carswell, 2014)

- *Feeney's Canadian Law of Wills*, 4th ed. (LexisNexis Canada Inc., 2016)

- *The Canadian Law of Unjust Enrichment and Restitution* (LexisNexis Canada Inc., 2014)

- *Contesting a Will without a Lawyer* (yes, this book!) (Self-Counsel Press, 2018)

3. Where Do I Find Secondary Sources?

Your best bet for doing your initial legal research is a law library, simply because they have the best selection of secondary materials. Their materials are used by lawyers and law students so you can be confident that they are accurate, local, and appropriate. You will find law libraries at courthouses and law schools, and you may find a good selection of legal materials in larger public libraries. Most libraries have online catalogs so you can search online before making the trip to the library. Once you know which cases you want to look for, you can search for them online or through the law books themselves. The best online source of cases and legislation in Canada is www.CanLII.org, a free legal research website that is funded and run by the provincial law societies.

Law librarians are gold mines of information; let them know exactly the topic (or reference book) you want to look at and they will guide you. You may not be allowed to check out the books from the library if you are not a lawyer or law student.

There are some excellent legal research software packages available so that you can do your legal research online, but because of the expense they are rarely owned by anyone other than lawyers, law schools, and law libraries.

4. What Is Precedent?

Precedent literally means "what went before." In the context of litigation, precedent refers to the idea of the court following cases that have been decided in the past. This is done so that cases with similar facts will have similar outcomes even when the cases are decided by different judges in different places. There can be some certainty among lawyers and laypeople alike as to what will happen when any given case goes to court.

For example, let's look at the case of *Pecore v. Pecore*, decided by the Supreme Court of Canada in 2007. In that case, a father added his daughter to his bank account and investment account, making her a joint owner. The question the court was asked to decide was whether on the death of the father, the joint assets belonged to the daughter or to the father's estate. The court confirmed that the presumption of resulting trust arose, as we discussed earlier in this book. The court examined the facts of the case and found that there was very strong evidence that the father intended the account to be a gift to his daughter.

Since the Pecore case was decided it has been cited in at least 500 reported cases. It gives guidance to everyone who is working on a case with joint assets because it describes how to tell where the asset really belongs. If your case was about joint assets, you could look up the Pecore case and find out what "strong evidence" the court relied on. If you

can find the same sort of strong evidence for your case, you could expect a similar outcome.

In our legal system, we are required to follow the precedents that our courts have set down for us, as long as we ensure that the facts and the legal questions we are following are the same as the cases we are working on. This is one of the cornerstones of the common law legal system that exists in all Canadian provinces and territories except Quebec.

To use precedent cases, you must find ones that have similar facts to your case and which talked about similar issues to your case. For example, you might be bringing a lawsuit to enforce a promise that was made to you by someone who is now deceased. You want to find cases that had the outcome you want, and to show that you should have the same outcome because your case is similar. If the asset you were promised is a farm, find cases that dealt with promises made regarding farms. If you passed up job opportunities to help on the farm, find other cases in which the plaintiff passed up job opportunities to help on the farm. The more your facts look like those in the precedent case, the better your chance of getting the same outcome as those cases.

The following are some general rules about how to use precedent cases properly:

1. The level of court that decided the precedent case is important. The higher the court, the more persuasive the case. Remember, the Court of Appeal can overturn cases from superior court, so it outranks the superior court. The Supreme Court of Canada can overturn Courts of Appeal, so it outranks all courts.

2. The province or territory of the precedent case matters, too. Try to find

cases that were decided in your province because laws and rules vary across the country. You may find cases from other provinces that have the result you want, but you run the risk that the judge will question whether that procedure is followed in your province. Keep it local if you possibly can.

3. Cases that are recent are better than cases that are outdated. You do not want to risk using old cases and later realizing the law has changed so the cases are no longer relevant. You will notice that in estate litigation, some important precedent cases date back more than 100 years. Though these cases are definitely not recent, they have been mentioned and relied on in recent cases and are therefore still considered relevant.

5. How Do I Know Which Cases Apply to Me?

To demonstrate how a case might be applied to another, I am using an excerpt (shown below) from an actual case found on www.canlii.org to show how to identify and use information on the first page of a published case. Knowing how to quickly summarize this material will help you find the right cases and discard the ones that you don't want. You could read each and every case in its entirety to see whether it applies to you, but that would take more hours than you likely have available.

At the top of the first page of each case you will see a heading similar to the one in Sample 3. From this information you know the name of the case, when it was published, which level of court heard the case, and how it is cited. As described above in the section on precedent, the location and date of the

case are important. When you prepare your brief, you must include the citation for each case so that the court can also see the information about the date and place of the case.

There is a wealth of important information for you to look at in Sample 3. First, there is a brief summary of the facts of the case. This will help you determine which cases have facts similar to yours or looked at issues similar to yours. If you glance at the summary and see nothing there that seems to apply to your situation, you can skip the case and go on to another. If you do see information that is relevant to you, then you know you must look more closely at the case.

The next important section for you is the list of authorities cited. That refers to the cases ("authorities") that the lawyers put in front of the judge in this case to support their point. If you find that the case is relevant to your situation, then use the list of authorities to find more cases you can use. Each case will have slightly different facts but will all be focused on the topic raised. It would be particularly useful for you to read the case in front of you to see what the judge said about the cases brought to court by the lawyers. Which ones did the judges say they found especially helpful? This will give you ideas about arguments you can make in court and help you understand exactly how each case might help you.

Finally, you can see under the section called "texts considered" that the lawyers and the judge in this case relied on a secondary source. This can be very helpful and guide you to a book that discusses the very topic you need to learn about.

6. Is There Anyone Who Can Help Me with Legal Research?

There is no question that legal research can be challenging to someone who has not been

SAMPLE 3
CASE REPORT

IN THE SUPREME COURT OF NEWFOUNDLAND AND LABRADOR
TRIAL DIVISION (GENERAL)

Citation: Coombs v. Walsh (Estate), 2017 NLTD(G) 83
Date: April 28, 2017
Docket: 201601E14932

Following this information is a list of the parties who are involved in the litigation and the name of the judge who decided the case. Then there is a summary like this:

Summary:

Helen Walsh died on February 4, 2016, and Letters of Probate were granted on March 18, 2016. The majority of her Estate was bequeathed to two children, Veronica Brien and Francis Walsh. The Applicants who are also the children of Helen Walsh, filed an application on January 13, 2017, seeking revocation of probate alleging lack of testamentary capacity and undue influence. The Second and Third Respondents denied the allegations.

The Court found there was a genuine issue for trial and ordered revocation of probate and proof of the Will in solemn form. Costs of the application to be determined.

Appearances:

Ms. D. Lynne Butler	*Appearing on behalf of the Applicants*
Ms. Catherine J. Perry	*Appearing on behalf of the Respondents*

Authorities Cited:

*CASES CONSIDERED: **Garwood v. Garwood Estate,** 2007 MBCA 160 (CanLII); **Vout v. Hay**, 1995 CanLII 105 (SCC), [1995] 2 S.C.R. 876; **Verbonac Estate, Re** [indexed as **Milevoi v. Muzychyn** (1997), 1997 CanLII 17189 (SK QB), 159 Sask. R. 299, [1997] S.J. No. 565 (Q.B.)]; **Carlson v. Lazicki**, 2012 SKQB 260 (CanLII); **Kapacila Estate v. Otto**, 20120 SKCA 85, [2010] 9 W.W.R. 575; **Bermingham v. Bermingham Estate**, [2007] O.J. No. 1320, 32 E.T.R. (3d) 292 (Ont. S.C.); **Russell v. Frazer**, 1980 CanLII 737 (BC CA), [1980] B.C.J. No. 16, 8 E.T.R. 245.*

TEXTS CONSIDERED: Feeney's Canadian Law of Wills, 4th ed. (Markham: LexisNexis Canada Inc.).

trained in it. Law students are trained and coached and are given constant feedback on their research during the first few years of working because it can be a difficult skill to master. If you find it overwhelming, you are not alone. You might wish to get help with this stage of the process even if you intend to represent yourself in the courtroom on the hearing date.

If you seek help, be extremely careful about whom you rely on. It is a serious mistake to rely on someone who is not trained in the law and in legal research. Do not accept legal help from bankers, accountants, or financial advisors. While they are essential to certain estate tasks and may be experts on tax or other matters, they are not experts in legal research.

A pitfall that a large number of people fall into is relying on unsupervised legal assistants and paralegals. This happens frequently because it may seem that a person who works in a law office must know about the law. The situation is exacerbated by the frequent assertions by legal assistants that they actually do the legal work for the lawyer. Neither of those things is true, at least, not to the extent that you should stake your lawsuit on it. Legal assistants, and to some extent paralegals, do what they are told to do and are supervised by lawyers who take responsibility for the work. The decisions about what needs to be done is made by the lawyers. As a general rule, lawyers know the law and legal assistants know the forms. Though it may be tempting to rely on a legal assistant that you believe is experienced and knowledgeable, do not do so unless that person is trained and experienced in legal research.

If you are willing to pay someone to do the research for you, there are lawyers who spend their careers doing research on a contract basis. You might find it great value for the money when you consider not just the legal knowledge required to get the research right, but also the time you are likely to spend doing the research yourself. You would have the job done quickly with a great deal of confidence that it is done properly and thoroughly. Research lawyers are easier to find in larger metro areas than smaller communities, but it is worth a bit of searching time to see if you can find a lawyer who will do this work for you.

Along the same lines, you might well find a law student who is willing to do that research more cheaply than a lawyer would do it. Plenty of law students earn a bit of extra money and gain experience by doing law-related activities such as research. Though a student would not be as reliable as a lawyer (simply because the person has not yet had the opportunity to apply his or her research to many real clients) you would still have someone with legal research training to help you. If you live in a city with a law school, you could probably find someone within hours of posting a notice on a physical bulletin board. Anyone in Canada could probably find a suitable student by posting on a virtual notice board.

If you decide to hire a student, make sure that he or she is actually enrolled in the faculty of law and not in "pre-law." Anyone can say they are "pre-law" and over the years I have met students in everything from anthropology to zoology who call themselves" pre-law" because they plan one day to go to law school.

An online resource you might want to check out is *The Canadian Legal Research and Writing Guide*, which can be found at legalresearch.org. It includes a step-by-step legal research process for you to follow.

7. What Goes into the Memorandum of Law and Argument?

As you draft your Memorandum, keep in mind that you have already prepared an Affidavit that holds all the facts. You do not repeat them all in the Memorandum though there will be some overlap. Your purpose in the Memorandum is to show how the law applies to the facts and to persuade the judge that the law is in your favour.

The following are the general steps for drafting your litigation documents:

1. You draft and send a demand letter (see Chapter 14).

2. If you do not get a result after the demand letter, you draft and file a Statement of Claim and an Affidavit.

3. If you are given a court date for a chambers hearing, you do your legal research to define how the law applies to you.

4. You put your legal research and the facts you need into a Memorandum of Law and Argument.

In your Memorandum, you are going to identify the legal ground or issue that you are relying on, such as undue influence or unjust enrichment. Once you do that, you will talk about what the law and the cases say a person has to do to show that ground exists or to prove the case. Then you will refer to the facts in your Affidavit to show the court that your case fits and that you have met all the requirements.

You will have to refer to the specific laws, regulations, and cases that support you. Later in this chapter there is an explanation of how to cite a statute (that is, a written law) and a case.

You will also explain what it is you want the court to do (this is sometimes called the relief you want), such as remove the executor or set down the matter for trial. Before asking for any kind of relief, you should have covered in your Memorandum exactly why you are entitled to it.

This is the most difficult of all of the documents you will have to prepare. It will be slow going until you get used to the format of making a point and referring to the supporting law. Set aside enough time to organize your research and distill it into the points you need to make. Think through your case to decide how it should be organized; are there points that make more sense if they are raised after certain other points? Be prepared to do more than one draft of your Memorandum before deciding it is finished.

8. What Format Do I Use?

In this section, I will mention the general parts of a Memorandum of Law and Argument in the order in which they should appear in your document. This will give you a structure to get started and to keep yourself on track. I highly recommend preparing an outline using these parts of the Memorandum as your starting point and filling in smaller headings as you go. As you add each point to your outline, put the statutes and cases in order of the points they support. Refer to the sample Memorandum in Sample 4 for an example of how that part should look.

1. Introductory matters

2. Background facts

3. What has caused this matter to be in court: law and facts

4. Statements about why you think the other party is at fault

5. Statements about how you are affected by the situation

6. Request for relief

Even though you wrote your affidavit in the first person, the accepted way of writing a Memorandum of Law and Argument is to refer to yourself in the third person, as "the Plaintiff." This is mostly for the purpose of keeping the reader on track of who is supposed to have done what. Refer to Sample 4 to see how that is done.

8.1 Introductory matters

This section should be brief but informative. You will identify yourself as the Plaintiff. Also include relevant information such as your relationship to the deceased and to the Defendant. The facts of your case will determine what else you need to include. For example, in an application to pass accounts, you identify yourself as a beneficiary of the estate. If you have covered this in your Affidavit, you do not need to go into great detail in your Memorandum.

8.2 Background facts

Again, keep this section brief because there is already an affidavit in place that provides the details. In this section, give the abbreviated version. For example, if in your affidavit you have described fully your many attempts to get information from the executor, you need not repeat yourself. You could give the short version by saying something like "despite the Plaintiff's best efforts, he has not been able to get information from the Defendant."

Also include a brief summary of what has happened with your case so far. For example, if you have been to chambers and an order was issued, mention it. If you have been through case management or mediation, state that as well.

8.3 What has caused this matter to be in court

Now you are going to get into the meat of your Memorandum. This is the section in which you are going to introduce the ground you're relying on, or the issue that needs to be decided. In this section you are arguing your case, so you should present the facts and law that support your case.

There will be some overlap with your affidavit in this section, because this is where the facts and the law meet. For example, in this section you might say that your grandmother made a will in 2017 but she had been diagnosed with dementia in 2009 and therefore you believe that she did not have testamentary capacity. Those are the facts you are relying on. You would then continue on to show what should happen now according to law. To carry on with our example of the grandmother, you might say that based on the law of testamentary capacity, your grandmother's will should be declared invalid.

Each time you make a statement about the law, refer to the statute or the case that supports that particular point. For example, let's say that you are bringing a lawsuit to declare a will invalid because it was not properly executed and witnessed and the testator did not have full knowledge of the contents of the will. One paragraph of your Memorandum might say (this example is based on Saskatchewan law):

1. In order for a will to be valid in this province, it has to meet certain requirements as set out in section 7(1) of the *Wills Act*, SS 1996, c W-14.1, including being signed in front of two witnesses.

2. The requirements in this case were not met because the will was only signed by one witness, and that witness is a beneficiary, namely John Jones.

In this example above, you have stated that you believe that section 7 of the *Wills Act* applies, so you will photocopy or print a copy of section 7. You should not copy the entire Act but you must include the entire section 7. You will note that, in Sample 4, below your paragraph you have mentioned "Tab 1." That is the notation that refers the judge to the tab holding the copy of section 7. Behind your Memorandum you will place each of the laws and cases you refer to, in order. In paragraph 2 you do not refer to a law or a case so you do not need a tab. Your affidavit should set out the whole story of the will and its witnessing by Mr. Jones.

To continue with our example, let's say that your next point is that although Saskatchewan has curative legislation, you don't believe it applies in this case. Your Memorandum might go on to say:

3. Section 37 of the *Wills Act* allows the court to declare that a will is valid if it substantially complies with the signing formalities. In this case, however, the Plaintiff submits that is not an appropriate step for the court to take because ...

You would then go on to include the facts of your case (which MUST be set out in your Affidavit) that show why the curative provisions do not apply. Under Tab 2 you would include a copy of section 37 of the Act. You would continue on in this way until you have addressed all of the issues and points that you feel are relevant to your case. You will find that about one-third to one-half of your points will need a tab.

8.4 Statements about why you think the other party is at fault

In this part of your Memorandum of Law and Argument, you will tell the court why you think the problem lies with the Defendant. If it's a case of undue influence, set out how you believe the Defendant unduly influenced the testator, giving the most specific examples that you can. It is not enough to say that someone was unduly influenced; you must prove who did that, and how he or she did it. If you are trying to compel an executor to pass his or her accounts, show what is wrong with the accounting you received and give specific examples of your efforts to get better information.

If there is more than one defendant, make sure you show how each is involved and how each is responsible for the situation.

In this part of your Memorandum, you may refer to cases and laws as you did in the previous section. You may also attach other attachments (exhibits) that prove your case. When you refer back to the Chapter 9, section 7, the section that talks about getting your best evidence, you will see that you might have correspondence, receipts, emails, medical reports, or a dozen other things that bit by bit, piece by piece, tell your story. You can attach any of those items using the same system as shown above; make a point and refer the judge to a tab holding your evidence. Just make sure you fully identify each piece of evidence in terms of what it is, when it was created, and where it came from.

8.5 Statements about how you are affected by the situation

So far, you have stated your issue and you have stated that you think the defendant is responsible for creating it. Now you must show how it affects you, and possibly how it affects other people, if that is relevant to your case. For example, you might say that the actions of the defendants have made it impossible to administer the estate so none of the beneficiaries have received their inheritance. Perhaps because of the fraudulent will, there have been delays and legal costs and family disharmony. The specifics of your document will of course depend on the circumstances of your case.

If you are alleging that you lost time off work or had to spend money because of the actions of the defendants, be specific. It is not sufficient to say you had to take "a lot of time" off work. Name the dates. Similarly, it is not enough to say that you spent "a lot of money" on matters arising from the lawsuit. You must give specific details.

You cannot make a claim for the kind of damages that are seen in most other types of civil litigation. This means that you cannot claim for items such as pain, suffering, or emotional trauma. While it is fine to mention these things and describe how the lawsuit has affected you emotionally, do not expect the judge to award you any money for that.

8.6 Request for relief

As mentioned, "relief" refers to the actions you want the judge to take to fix the situation, hopefully in your favour. You should list the things you want in point form and keep them brief and to the point. Here is an example:

Summary of relief sought:

1. The Plaintiff seeks an order removing the executor of the estate and replacing him with the Office of the Public Trustee.

2. The Plaintiff seeks the costs of this application against the Defendant.

Always put your request for costs at the very bottom of your list. To fill in the rest of the list, go to your Statement of Claim and make sure that all of the things you asked for there are also asked for in your Memorandum. All of your documents should be consistent in what you are requesting.

9. Tips on How Your Memorandum of Law and Argument Should Look

Here are a few tips for formatting your Memorandum of Law and Argument:

1. Your document should have a cardstock cover on the front in white, buff, or pale blue, and plain white paper inside.

2. Use 8½ by 11-inch, standard size paper. Do not use legal size. If one of the attachments is legal size, fold up the bottom of it so that the bottom does not extend beyond the regular pages.

3. Pages should be printed on one side only.

4. Your document should be Cerlox-bound or coil-bound unless it is thin enough to be stapled together.

5. Use black ink in a plain, easy-to-read font.

6. Do not type in all caps, though you may use all caps for headings.

7. Use either double spaces, or one and a half spaces between lines.

8. Use headings in bold type or underlined to organize topics within your document.

9. Use point form for lists.

10. Number all paragraphs.

11. Number the pages.

12. Use a left-justified margin with a ragged right edge margin.

13. Decide whether you are going to start each paragraph with an indent or not, and use that style consistently throughout the document.

14. Check and double-check your spelling.

15. When typing dollar amounts, leave off the "00" at the end. For example, say $1,000 not $1,000.00.

16. Keep your sentences short.

17. After the cardstock cover, put in the Memorandum in its entirety, then add the copies of the laws and cases behind the Memorandum. The laws and cases should appear in the order in which they are mentioned in your Memorandum.

18. Include an index for the laws and cases, inserted after the Memorandum and before the copies of the laws and cases.

19. Put numbered tabs on the laws and cases that correspond to the numbers you assign them in the Memorandum.

Remember that the more complex the document, the more you must organize the material to ensure that you are telling a coherent story and getting your points across. Do not jump around from topic to topic and back again. Group all of your points about one topic together under one heading, and use subheadings if that helps you (and the reader) navigate around the document. Make your document as easy to follow as possible.

10. How to Include Statutes and Cases in Your Memorandum

As you have seen from the previous sections of this chapter, whenever you refer to a case in your Memorandum of Law and Argument, you have to include the citation. This refers to information that tells the reader when the case took place, where it took place, and where to find it. The judge wants to see that information for every case you rely on in your Memorandum. Cases may be reported in a geographical area, such as cases from a single province. Cases are also sometimes reported in groups that cover certain topics, such as trusts or estates. Sometimes they are even organized in terms of the court that heard them, particularly if the case was heard at the Supreme Court of Canada, our country's highest court.

Fortunately, you don't have to figure out the citation on your own. Every case comes with it already attached and all you need to do is copy it directly from the case. If you look back at the sample case of *Coombs v. Walsh* that was shown in Sample 3, you will notice that right below the title it says "Citation: *Coombs v. Walsh (Estate)*, 2017 NLTD(G) 83." This citation shows the name of the parties (Coombs, Walsh), the year the case was heard (2017), the province and level of court that heard it [Newfoundland and Labrador Trial Division (General)] and where to find it [page 83 of the NLTD(G) reports for that year]. If you cannot find the citation directly under the title of the case you want to use, keep looking because the citation will be somewhere near the top of the first page. Some reports use slightly different formats but they will all be there.

Statutes (written laws) also have citations that contain a lot of vital information. Here is an example: *Wills Act*, RSY 2002, c 230. This brief blurb tells us the name of the law (the Wills Act), the province it applies to (Y is for Yukon), and where to find it (RSY means "revised statutes of Yukon" and c. 230 means chapter 230 in the book of Yukon statutes). Again, you must use the citation for every statute you refer to in your Memorandum. You can generally find the citation for a statute at the very top of the first page and at the very end of the last page.

Here is an example of citations being used in a Memorandum of Law and Argument.

---

1. The Plaintiffs are seeking costs against the Defendant personally on a solicitor and own client basis due to the Defendant's failure to administer the estate in a proper manner and her vindictive behaviour towards all parties. While this form of costs is not the norm for estates, the Plaintiffs submit that it is an appropriate remedy in this case. The general rule for awarding costs on this basis was set down by the Supreme Court of Canada in *Young v. Young*, 1993 CanLII 34 (SCC), [1993] 4 S.C.R. 3., where it was held that solicitor-client costs "are generally awarded only where there has been reprehensible, scandalous or outrageous conduct on the part of one of the parties."

2. This Honourable Court examined the meaning of the words "reprehensible, scandalous or outrageous" in *Perry v. Heywood* (1998), 1998 CanLII 18075 (NL SCTD), 175 Nfld. & P.E.I.R. 253 (Nfld. T.D.) at para. 63, and said that:

   "[R]eprehensible" is a word of wide meaning. It can include conduct which is scandalous, outrageous or constitutes misbehaviour; but it also included milder forms of misconduct. It means simply "deserving of reproof or rebuke."

To see more examples of how to use the citations in your Memorandum, refer to Sample 4. Do not be concerned that your Memorandum seems to be much lengthier than the sample; it has been abbreviated.

SAMPLE 4
MEMORANDUM OF LAW AND ARGUMENT

Court file no. _____

IN THE SUPREME COURT OF NEWFOUNDLAND AND LABRADOR
TRIAL DIVISION (GENERAL)

BETWEEN:

GEORGE SMITH

APPLICANT

AND:

SHARON JONES
JOHN SMITH

RESPONDENTS

MEMORANDUM OF LAW AND ARGUMENT

1. The Respondents rely on the facts sworn to by Sharon Jones and John Smith filed in this action as well as additional facts as set out in this response.

2. In paragraph 32 of the Applicant's materials, he states that Mrs. Smith did not instruct anyone to designate her five children as beneficiaries of her account. However, this would seem directly contradictory to the understanding of her investment advisor, Mr. Carletto. He mentioned those particular instructions several times in his letter. In fact, he identified this as Mrs. Smith's primary concern. He states in his letter (page four, paragraph 3) that he "was being harshly accused of wrongdoings that never occurred."

Tab 1

3. George Smith's position is and has consistently been that the beneficiaries of the accounts are all five of Mrs. Smith's children, and not the estate of Mrs. Smith.

4. The Applicant states at paragraph 14 that because he is named as residuary beneficiary in the will of Mrs. Smith, he is entitled to receive the proceeds of the joint bank accounts. There is no law provided by the Applicant to support this statement and the Respondents submit that this is because there is no law that would support it. The Respondents submit that the bank accounts held jointly between Mrs. Smith and George Smith **do not** form part of the estate and therefore the terms of the will are, on this issue, immaterial.

5. The law on this point (***Pecore v. Pecore*** [2007] 1 S.C.R. 795, 2007 SCC; ***Madsen Estate v. Saylor*** [2007] 1 S.C.R. 838, 2007 SCC 18) and (***Sawdon Estate v. Sawdon***, 2014 ONCA 101) may be summarized as follows: Where an asset is held jointly between a parent and a child, there is a rebuttable presumption that the asset is held in trust for the estate of the parent unless the surviving joint owner can

produce evidence to rebut the presumption. The presumption is rebutted by evidence of the parent's intention that the asset should not form part of the estate.

Tab 2

6. The Respondents submit that there is ample evidence of Mrs. Smith's intentions that will serve to rebut the presumption, to wit:

   a. Letters from two banking officers confirming that Mrs. Smith told them she wanted the accounts to be paid to all of her children upon her death; and

   b. Statements from John Smith to the effect that Mrs. Smith told him that he was being added as a joint owner so that he could distribute the funds to all of the siblings after her death.

7. The Respondents therefore submit that the joint bank accounts do not fall into the estate of Mrs. Smith but should be paid to John Smith to be distributed equally to all five of the children of Mrs. Smith.

8. The Respondents are seeking costs against the Applicant personally on a solicitor and own client basis due to the Applicant's failure to administer the estate in a proper manner and his continually dragging all parties through repeated, pointless legal and administrative procedures. While this form of costs is not the norm for estates, the Respondents submit that it is an appropriate remedy in this case. The general rule for awarding costs on this basis was set down by the Supreme Court of Canada in *Young v. Young*, 1993 CanLII 34 (SCC), [1993] 4 S.C.R. 3., where it was held that solicitor-client costs "*are generally awarded only where there has been reprehensible, scandalous or outrageous conduct on the part of one of the parties.*"

Tab 3

9. This Honourable Court examined the meaning of the words "reprehensible, scandalous or outrageous" in *Perry v. Heywood* (1998), 1998 CanLII 18075 (NL SCTD), 175 Nfld. & P.E.I.R. 253 (Nfld. T.D.) at para. 63, and said that:

   > … "*[R]eprehensible*" *is a word of wide meaning. It can include conduct which is scandalous, outrageous or constitutes misbehaviour; but it also included milder forms of misconduct. It means simply "deserving of reproof or rebuke.*"

Tab 4

10. The Respondents submit that the actions of the Applicant are outrageous and deserving of reproof or rebuke. The estate has remained unsettled for more than four years because the Applicant/Executor:

    a. Continues to put his own financial interests ahead of those of the estate;

    b. Continues to waste time and resources by continually bringing legal actions and administrative complaints that do not advance the estate but are designed to intimidate and frustrate other parties and advance his own interests; and

   c. Has been unsuccessful in ALL of his malicious and frivolous legal applications, administrative complaints, and attempted criminal charges, yet the Respondents have borne all of their own legal costs to date.

11. The Respondents submit that the Applicant should be discouraged from continuing to waste court, police, administrative, and the Respondents' personal resources by a court order of solicitor and own client costs against him.

<u>Summary of relief sought:</u>

12. The Respondents reiterate the relief sought in their earlier materials that the Applicant be removed as the executor of the estate and replaced with the Office of the Public Trustee.

13. The Respondents seek a declaration that the joint bank account held by Mrs. Smith and her son, George Smith, is to be paid to George Smith on the condition that he share the account proceeds equally among all five of the children of Mrs. Smith.

14. The Respondents seek the costs of this application against the Applicant on a solicitor-client basis.

_____

Your signature

Your name
Respondent

Whose address for service is:

TO:
State the name and address of the opposing party, or his or her lawyer.

12
Cross-examination on Affidavits

The terms examination and discovery refer to a set of processes that involve cross-examining various people who are involved in your lawsuit. A cross-examination means asking a witness more questions about the evidence that he or she has given to get a more in-depth answer than has been provided. You do not cross-examine your own witnesses; you will, however, probably want to cross-examine the witnesses who are on the other side of your lawsuit. Of course, the other side may wish to cross-examine you and your witnesses as well.

It is not mandatory for you to cross-examine witnesses. It is your right to do so but only if you feel it is going to be worthwhile. The judge will not draw any negative meaning from the fact that you don't want to cross-examine anyone. If the people on the other side of the lawsuit want to cross-examine you on your affidavit, you cannot refuse without facing legal consequences.

1. Why Cross-examine?

There are multiple reasons for cross-examining someone about evidence he or she has already given. They are to —

- find out more detail about the person's evidence so that you are sure that you know his or her whole story;

- get copies of documents or photos that he or she has yet to produce;

- determine whether there is any common ground that might lead to a settlement; and

- find something wrong with his or her evidence so that you can discredit the person. This could be catching him or her in a lie or exaggeration, or causing the person to contradict himself or herself.

An affidavit is the usual way that evidence is given in chambers. Although chambers is a courtroom and there is a judge present, it is intended to be used for hearings and applications that are not full trials, as discussed in Chapter 7 of this book. In chambers, only the lawyer or the self-represented person speaks to the judge. Any information given by the witnesses or the parties to the matter is written down, sworn before a commissioner for oaths, and presented in the form of an affidavit to the other side.

The affidavit becomes the basis for the arguments you make in court. You will already have prepared a Memorandum of Law and Argument (sometimes called a brief) that ties together the facts in your affidavit and the relevant law. You can only make arguments based on the facts in the affidavits. If any important facts have been left out, you cannot talk about them. This means that if you believe the whole story has not been told, you need to find a way to get those facts into court. That's where your cross-examination comes in. Whatever the witness says in the cross-examination becomes information you can use in court.

Because the evidence is written down and not given orally in front of the judge, you will not have the opportunity to cross-examine the witnesses in court with the judge present. The right to cross-examine witnesses is an integral part of our legal system, so you have the right to cross-examine the witnesses whose evidence has been made into an affidavit.

2. When Are Cross-examinations Done?

In the context of estate litigation, there are two main types of examinations that may arise:

1. The examination of a witness who has given evidence in a sworn affidavit.

2. Cross-examination of a witness in court during a trial.

Not many litigated estates make it all the way to a full trial but yours could be one of them, so it is possible that you might have to cross-examine someone in that context. It is much more likely that you will cross-examine someone on his or her affidavit evidence, which is done in a much different setting. Although we will focus more on cross-examination on affidavits in this chapter, you should use the same steps when preparing your questions for trial as you do for preparing for examinations on affidavits.

If you are cross-examining during a trial, you will do your examination in the court room when your witness is called to the stand. If you are cross-examining on an affidavit, the session is held at a time that is pre-scheduled to suit everyone's schedules. They must take place after the judge or trial coordinator has set a trial date but before the matter goes to trial.

3. Where Are Cross-examinations Held?

Cross-examinations on affidavits are normally held in a lawyer's office in a private conference room. If you are not using a lawyer for your litigation, you will have to find a similar location. If the people on the other side of the lawsuit are working with a lawyer, you might be able to use that lawyer's office.

If that is not possible, talk to the staff at your local courthouse to see whether there is a conference room or interview room you can book for your cross-examination. Another possibility is the office of the company that supplies the court reporters for your cross-examination, if you live in a jurisdiction where the reporters are not supplied by the courts themselves. The company might provide a conference room for clients who need a central, professional location. If all else fails, try contacting local business hotels to see if they will rent you a small conference room for the time you need.

It is acceptable to hold your session at any location that both parties agree to use, but you will want to make sure that the location offers privacy and is comfortable enough to spend many hours or even a few days in.

4. What Is the Procedure for a Cross-examination?

The basic procedure for cross-examination is as follows:

1. All parties assemble in the agreed-on location a few minutes before the scheduled start time. Do not discuss the case with the witness or his or her lawyer at this time.

2. The court reporter arrives and sets up his or her equipment at the head of the table.

3. The witness and his or her lawyer sit on one side of the table and you sit at the other side, facing them.

4. You get out your materials and get ready to write down the answers.

5. When the court reporter is ready, he or she will ask everyone to identify themselves for the record.

6. When the court reporter says, "we are on the record" or "I'm recording now," what is being said in the room is being recorded as part of the evidence given and will show up on a transcript later.

7. The court reporter will ask the witness to swear under oath to tell the truth.

8. The court reporter will ask you to state which affidavit you're examining on, at which point you'll say the name of the witness and the day it was signed.

9. You will start asking your questions and the witness will answer.

10. There may occasionally be brief breaks if the court reporter needs to adjust equipment, if the witness needs to ask his or her lawyer a question, or if you and the other party need a moment to clarify something between you.

11. When you have asked all of the questions you intend to ask the witness, you tell the court reporter that you have finished.

12. When you finish off, say that you are adjourning the session subject to the undertakings. This reserves the right for you to come back and examine further if the witness fails to provide the undertakings that he or she promises.

5. Who May Do Cross-examinations?

You or your lawyer may conduct a cross-examination of a witness. Do not ask a friend or colleague to do this for you, as the person to be cross-examined does not have to submit to a cross-examination by anyone but you or your lawyer.

6. Who Can Be Cross-examined?

Anybody who has filed an affidavit in support of the lawsuit can be examined by the opposing party. This includes you, if you are the plaintiff.

You can cross-examine anyone from the opposing side of your lawsuit who has given an affidavit. This might be the defendant, other family members, medical doctors, expert witnesses, or those giving supporting statements such as bankers, social workers, or lawyers. You can cross-examine everyone on the other side if you believe that will help your case, but usually you will only examine those you feel will be the most useful. Usually this means cross-examining the people whose affidavits contain the evidence that is most harmful to you or whose affidavits hint at situations without giving full information. You do not have to cross-examine anyone if you do not wish to do so.

You would schedule only one witness to be cross-examined at a time. Normally examinations are scheduled in blocks of half-days. If you only have a few questions, you would book a half-day, which would be a morning or an afternoon depending on when everyone is available. It always takes longer than you think it will because of all of the setting up and preliminary matters. If you want to ask lots of questions, book at least a full day. You might even book two or three days and if it doesn't take as long as expected, you can cancel the last day or half-day.

There is normally a lunch break of an hour taken in the middle of the day. This can be adjusted as long as everyone is in agreement. Though you may think that it would be better simply to power straight through without a break, I recommend that you take the lunch break anyway. Use the time to stretch your legs and refresh yourself mentally. You will be sharper after the break if you use it wisely.

Also during the break, think about the answers you've heard so far. Try to summarize how the witness is behaving. Ask yourself how you would describe this witness if you had to tell someone on the phone how it was going. Would you say that the witness is cooperative? Sullen? Talkative? Hostile?

Tearful? Use that summary to decide whether you need to change anything about the way you are asking questions. Look at your notes to see whether there is any topic already covered that you need to touch on again.

7. What May I Ask?

You are entitled to ask questions about anything raised in the witness' affidavit. You can also ask anything raised in the affidavits of other witnesses if you believe this witness might somehow be involved in it. For example, if a doctor filed an affidavit talking about his diagnosis of dementia of the witness's father, you could ask about the witness's familiarity with that diagnosis.

There is an important distinction between direct examination and cross-examination that will affect what you ask about and how you ask your questions. A direct examination takes place when you are asking your own witnesses questions in front of a judge. Your purpose is to get their story to the judge in their own words. In direct examination, you have to be very careful not to lead the witness, or in other words, to put words in the witness's mouth. For example, you could not say to your own witness, "You thought Jane was pushing your mother to get a new will in her favour, didn't you?" You have to ask open-ended questions such as, "What was your impression of Jane's actions?"

Remember, when you are examining witnesses on their affidavits, you are not doing a direct examination; you are doing a cross-examination. The rules for how you must treat the witness are much different. In a cross-examination, you are allowed to ask leading questions. Most likely you will ask plenty of them. You are allowed to ask Jane, "Were you pushing your mother to get a new will in your favour?" She is not your witness and you are there to get the answers you need, so this type of question is the standard type.

If the witness you're examining has a lawyer, you can expect the lawyer to object to your questions from time to time, just as one would in a courtroom. However, there is no judge there to rule on the objection, so the parties have to figure it out themselves. Usually if a lawyer objects, he or she will state the objection then turn to the court reporter and ask to go off the record. This means the court reporter stops recording anything until the two sides have talked about what they are going to do about the objection. When everyone is ready to get going again, the lawyer will instruct the court reporter to go back on the record.

As you ask your questions, you might find that you feel some pressure to hurry things along. This is not surprising, given that everyone else in the room is watching you and waiting for your next question. Try to control the pace of the cross-examination so that it suits you. Take the time you need to write down the answers you're given. Ask for clarification of something if you need to. Take the time to read your next question and any reminders you wrote to yourself. Do not allow yourself to be rushed; it is your right to cross-examine the witness and you may not get another chance.

8. Preparing in Advance to Cross-examine a Witness

Preparing for your cross-examination of a witness will take some time. Don't expect to go into the session and "wing it." Even lawyers with many years of experience prepare carefully and thoroughly for a cross-examination. While you are in the cross-examination, you will need your list of questions, your list of potential undertakings, the affidavit filed by the witness, and a place to record the answers you get. All of this should be in one organized place, which you may refer to as your examination book.

A very handy way to set up your book is in a three-ring binder, but you may prepare any form that you can work with. It can be electronic if you are able to find and record information quickly in that format. The format is completely up to you as you are the only person who will be using it and you may do whatever works best for you.

Use methods of organization that will be simple to use such as the following:

1. Numbering your questions

2. Numbering your pages

3. Headings

4. Different colours

5. Tabs in your examination book to separate one witness' evidence from another

6. Tabs or flags on parts of the affidavit you will refer to

If you are going to cross-examine more than one witness, make a separate book for each one, or at least give each witness his or her own section so that you do not mix up the answers.

9. What Goes into My Examination Book?

To begin your examination book, start with question pages. Each page of your book should be divided lengthwise so that it has two equal halves. On the left you will prepare your questions, notes, and reminders to yourself, and your list of undertakings. You will leave the right-hand side blank until you are actually in the cross-examination; you will make notes about the witness's answers on the right. A sample of an examination book page is shown in Sample 5.

On the very first page of your book, on the top left, write the name of the person who is being examined. Below that write the court file number and the date of the affidavit you are examining. You will want that information at hand because the Court Reporter will ask you to state that information for the record before you start asking questions of the witness.

Below that, also on the left, begin writing the questions you want to ask. Number them. Try to set your questions so that you cover one topic thoroughly before moving to another topic, rather than jumping back and forth between topics. A logical organization of the questions will help you stay on track and will reduce the likelihood of confusion of the witness.

Some of your questions will have undertakings attached to them. This is explained in more detail later in this chapter. When a question leads to an undertaking, list the proposed undertaking below the question. Highlight it in some manner, such as using a different colour font, or simply by using a manual highlighting pen.

After your question pages, set up a separate page with the heading "undertakings given." Put a tab on that page so that you can flip back and forth to it several times during the cross-examination because you will need it several times. Every time you ask for an undertaking (more on undertakings in section 10.) and the witness agrees, record it on that

SAMPLE 5
EXAMINATION BOOK PAGE

Cross-examination of Mary Simms Court file no. 2019-010203 Affidavit filed July 21, 2019	
1. Are you the Mary Simms who swore an affidavit on July 21, 2019?	
2. I'm showing you paragraph 3 of that affidavit in which you said that several doctors said that your father didn't have capacity to make a will. What are the names of those doctors?	
3. Do you have letters or reports from any of those doctors?	
UNDERTAKING "A": Ask for copies of all letters and reports from the doctors Mary mentions.	
4. Why didn't you attach those reports to your affidavit? Is it because the reports don't actually say your father has dementia?	

page. Read the next section of this chapter to understand what information you should record. Once you have set up that page ready for use, set up another page headed "undertakings refused." On this page you will record every instance in which you asked for an undertaking but the witness refused to give it.

Behind the undertakings pages, place a copy of the affidavit about which you will be examining. Make a separate copy so that you can write on it, circle items, place sticky flags on it, and otherwise use it as a working tool during the cross-examination. Also add affidavits from other witnesses if you want to ask this witness about matters raised in those affidavits.

Then add several pages of blank paper, a couple of pens, and a highlighter. Your book is ready to be used.

10. What Is an Undertaking?

In the context of cross-examinations on affidavits, an undertaking is a promise to produce something. Note that this is not something you can do with cross-examination of a witness on the stand during a trial.

Let's say that you have started a lawsuit to compel an executor to pass his accounts. You have been trying to get important information for months but the executor won't give it to you. In his affidavit, the executor swears that he purchased the car he is driving from the estate at fair market value but he doesn't produce a Bill of Sale, cancelled cheque, or any other proof of his purchase. Since that information is important to you and was discussed in the executor's affidavit, you are entitled to ask the executor to promise or undertake to give you a copy of whatever he has.

You would say to the executor, for example, "Do you undertake to provide me with a copy of the cancelled cheque you used to purchase the vehicle as well as a copy of the bank statement showing the deposit of the cheque?" This would be said to him during your cross-examination of him while he is under oath.

If the executor agrees to provide it, write it down on the list of undertakings you will be making during the cross-examination. Remember that the court reporter who is recording the session will have a record of this undertaking as well, so now you have a promise made under oath to give you the information you want. If the executor refuses to provide the information you have requested, you will later be able to say to the judge that you asked for proof and the executor refused to give it so you are concluding there is no such proof. In this way, you weaken his argument that the car was properly purchased.

Some tips for getting worthwhile and effective undertakings from someone you are cross-examining:

1. Remember that you can only ask for documents, photographs, or information; you cannot ask for physical items, money, or other tangibles.

2. Be as precise as possible when describing the item you are asking for. If it is a letter or receipt, mention the date of it. If it is a work order, invoice, or other document that has a number, mention the number. If you are not precise enough, the person you are asking might say that he or she did not understand what you wanted and therefore was entitled to ignore your request.

3. Put a timeline on the request. For example, when you ask for the undertaking,

ask that the person get the item to you (or your lawyer) within two weeks. Anything that the person already has in his possession should be available immediately while something that he or she has to get from a bank or registry might take a bit longer. Be prepared that when you ask for the undertaking, it is alright if the person replies that he or she can do as you ask but will need a certain amount of time to obtain it. Just make sure that the request is not completely open-ended as to time. Also make sure that all undertakings have time to be completed before any court dates that are in place.

4. Be specific as to how the information is going to get to you. You can request that you receive items by way of email, fax, regular mail, registered mail, delivery, or whatever method best suits the situation.

5. Do not expect to obtain original documents. Photocopies will have to do in almost every case.

6. The person you are cross-examining (or his or her lawyer) should also be making a list of the undertakings. It is acceptable to compare lists informally after the session has wound up, just to ensure that everyone has the same understanding of what has been promised.

Within a day or two of the cross-examination being completed, write a letter to the person you cross-examined, or to his or her lawyer if he or she has one. Include a list of the items the person agreed to provide. Remind him or her of the timeline and the method of delivery.

11. How Do I Decide on My Questions?

The first question you will ask during the cross-examination is to request that the witness confirm that he or she is the person who swore the affidavit on which you're cross-examining. You may want to ask a few simple questions to get started and get comfortable. For example, if you want to ask a few factual questions such as, "How are you related to the deceased?" then by all means, do so.

There is no need to cross-examine on every paragraph of an affidavit if you are not going to gain anything from doing so. Most cross-examinations of a single witness take at least a day to complete, and nobody really wants it to take any longer than necessary. A better idea for choosing your questions is to read the affidavit over a couple of times until you feel familiar with the contents, then consider the following:

1. Is there anything in the affidavit that would damage your position if the judge believes it? It is highly likely that there will be, since the purpose of their affidavit is to present the opposite side of your story. Pick out the main points that you believe could damage your story and prepare questions that will force the witness to defend his or her position. For example, if you are claiming that a joint bank account belongs to you but the witness swears that your mother had said dozens of times that she was putting your name on her bank account because she wanted you to share it with the other kids, make the witness prove it. When did your mother say it? To whom did she say it? Who was there? Have those people stepped forward to swear this is true? Did your mother ever say it in

writing and if so, where is a copy of it? Is there any third-party support for the witness' position? The point is to make his or her statement sound weaker and less believable.

2. Is there anything in the affidavit that is simply untrue? If so, once again you want to ask questions that will make it clear that the item is untrue. Ask the witness what evidence he or she has to prove it's true. If you can cast doubt on the honesty of the witness, or on his or her clarity of recollection, you may be able to sway the judge into believing your version of the facts.

3. Does the witness contradict himself or herself in the affidavit? Is there anything in the affidavit that is an exaggeration or twisting of the truth? If so, point out the contradiction or exaggeration and ask the witness questions about it. Avoid asking open-ended questions such as "please explain this" because that simply gives the witness a chance to improve his or her position. Instead, you want to ask questions that suggest the witness might be lying or simply be completely mistaken about what really happened. Again, the idea is to damage the witness' credibility so that the judge does not accept his or her evidence.

4. Is there a subject mentioned in the affidavit that you simply need to know more about? If you need to know more about something that was mentioned, this is your chance to find out what you need. Ask for details such as names, dates, or places. If a report or a statement or some other documentation is referred to and you do not have a copy of it, ask for one. Find out who else was present at an event or was involved in an incident.

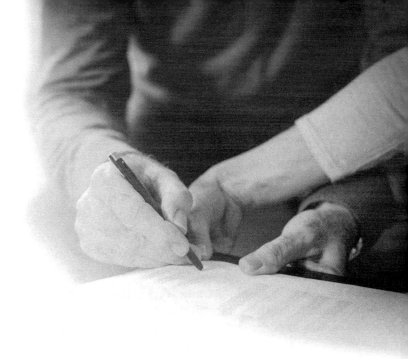

13
Costs

The word "costs" refers to the money you've had to pay out to conduct your lawsuit. It includes legal fees (if you use a lawyer) as well as out-of-pocket expenses such as court filing fees, photocopying, court reporter's fees, and so on. It does not include any compensation for time taken off work, lost wages, stress, or upset. Those items are referred to as damages, and you cannot ask for them in this type of litigation. It is strictly about recovering the funds you laid out to sue someone. In this chapter, we will look at the general rules of costs in estate litigation and talk about how and when to ask the court to award costs to you. (To learn even more about costs, refer to some of the secondary research sources mentioned in Chapter 11.)

The main thing to understand about getting the judge to award you your costs is that if you paid a lawyer, you are not going to recover every dollar you spent. It is rare that a judge will order that any party to litigation is going to be fully reimbursed for everything spent.

1. Can I Get Legal Aid?

Legal Aid is a government-funded program in which people who qualify for the program are provided with the assistance of a lawyer at little or no cost. To qualify for the programs you must be unable to afford a lawyer on your own. I know of no provinces or territories in which Legal Aid covers estate-related litigation.

2. Will the Other Side Cover My Costs?

The general rule for estate litigation is much the same as for any other litigation in Canada: The loser pays. This means if you win in court, you have the right to ask for costs against the people who lost. If you reach a settlement with someone regarding a legal battle, your settlement should include an agreement about who is paying costs for whom.

Like most rules, this general rule has some leeway in the hands of the judge, who can do what he or she thinks is fair in any given situation. Estate litigation is unlike other cases because of the existence of the estate itself. In most kinds of court battles there is one party who is suing a second party, and if one loses he or she can expect to pay the winner from his or her own resources. However, in an estate, there is a winner and a loser but there is also that third entity, the estate itself, which is sometimes available to pay the costs for one or both parties.

Years ago, almost all estate litigation was paid from the estate in question. Both sides could expect to have some or all of their costs covered even if it meant there was nothing left in the estate for the beneficiaries. As you can imagine, this was extremely unfair to the beneficiaries of the estate who were not involved but ended up losing because of someone else's battle. Because of this unfairness, over time the custom of using the estate to pay for costs has diminished greatly. The courts in Canada now take the position that the estate is not available as a fund for litigation except in unusual circumstances. Unfortunately, a lot of people still think they will get their costs covered by the estate and are as a result much more willing to fight things out to the bitter end.

It's important to understand that if you have conducted your lawsuit entirely without the help of lawyers, there is not much for you to recover in terms of costs. Since you do not have lawyer's fees to claim, your claim for costs would only include disbursements (including experts' fees, witness fees, court fees, and out-of-pocket expenses such as photocopies). Witness fees are nominal amounts expressed as per diems that a litigant must pay to a witness for his or her time and trouble. The amount is set out in provincial regulations. If the witness is an expert, (i.e., someone who is there simply because of his or her professional expertise), a litigant will

probably have to pay a large fee (hundreds of dollars) for a report and his or her time.

3. What If I'm the Executor?

In this book, we are focusing on launching and carrying out a lawsuit against an estate. As we discussed in the section on Conflict of Interest in Chapter 1, you should not be both an executor and the person who is challenging the will. If for some reason you are both, it is unlikely that a court would pay your costs from the estate to challenge the will when your job as executor is to defend the will.

If you are an executor who is not starting a lawsuit but is representing an estate that is being sued by someone else, the estate will most likely cover your costs. It is always up to the judge to decide on a case-by-case basis so there is never a guarantee that costs will be covered, but we do have some general rules that can offer some predictability.

If the lawsuit is one that is brought to determine the meaning of words in a will or for advice on how to deal with a situation, you as executor will almost certainly have your costs covered by the estate. This is because it was necessary for you to bring the matter to court and the executor is supposed to be indemnified for the expense of carrying out the estate; it's not supposed to put you out of pocket to do your job. If you cannot do your job without the assistance of the court to interpret a clause or to make other decisions about what is meant or intended by the will itself, there is no reason you should pay for that assistance personally. The general rule is that an executor is indemnified for legal fees in the normal course of an estate when the lawsuit is for the benefit of the estate.

If a beneficiary brings an application to contest the will on the basis of undue influence or incapacity (assuming that you are not the person accused of carrying out such undue influence), you as executor will have to represent the estate through the litigation. You will likely be awarded costs from the estate whether or not the application is successful. You were obligated to defend the will even though you were not responsible for its contents so generally you are not expected to cover those costs yourself.

If the lawsuit is one that involves the executor's conduct, the situation is less predictable. The example about approaching the court for assistance with interpretation of the will does not have anything to do with whether or not the executor is doing a good job. Things are very different when the reason the estate is in court is that someone is alleging fraud, negligence, or other misbehaviour by the executor.

If a beneficiary brings an application to remove an executor and can prove that the executor has behaved in a way that merits him or her being removed, then the court is probably not going to allow the estate to pay for the executor's costs. Why should the estate indemnify someone for maltreatment of the estate?

If you, as executor, have to bring an application to pass your accounts and if you do successfully pass them, you can expect the estate to cover your costs. That's because by passing your accounts, the court agrees that all of your transactions are in order and are approved, so you have done nothing wrong.

As you can see, it is not easy to rely on the costs rules because their outcome depends on the facts and details of each case. There is always the chance that the judge won't agree with any given request for costs. The unpredictability of costs awards is just one of the reasons that working out a settlement in the majority of cases may be a better choice than a full court battle.

4. How and When Do I Ask for Costs?

Costs are requested in court at the end of proceedings. Sometimes the judge will award costs without specifically being asked and in some cases the judge will ask the parties in court if they would like to address the issue of costs. In other cases, it might not be brought up at all if you do not bring it up yourself. Don't assume anything. You should be prepared to speak about costs and to ask for them if that is appropriate.

In chambers, you may hear the judge say that there will be costs in the cause. This means that the judge is not going to make a decision based on what happened in chambers that day. The judge wants costs to be awarded on the day the final hearing is done. This is because many of the applications in chambers are about interim matters or steps along the way to the final destination. The judge wants to keep the costs issue simple by saying it will be decided when we know who has won the lawsuit.

5. How Much of My Bill Is Covered If I Win Costs?

If you win your lawsuit in court and the judge awards you costs, you will have to prepare a document called a Bill of Costs. This is a document that summarizes what steps were taken in the lawsuit and tells how much you are claiming for each of the steps. The amount you will claim is not the full amount you paid to your lawyer, if you used a lawyer. The amounts are determined by a schedule that is published as part of the law of your province or territory (in the Rules of Court). The purpose of claiming costs this way is to impose a standard on everyone so that everyone is treated equally in terms of recovering legal costs.

Though many readers of this book are not using a lawyer for their litigation, others are working with lawyers or worked with a lawyer for part of the lawsuit. Because of this, we are including full instructions on how to use a Bill of Costs in section 6.

The Bill of Costs also shows what out-of-pocket disbursements you spent along the way and allows you to claim reimbursement for them. You can claim every dollar of the disbursements you paid during the lawsuit, but you have to attach receipts. When the Bill of Costs is finished, you may be required to file the Bill of Costs at the courthouse so that it can be processed by an assessment officer. You will then present it to the lawyer or the party on the other side, who will then pay you the amount of money shown on the Bill of Costs.

6. How Do I Fill in a Bill of Costs?

The form of the Bill of Costs varies quite a bit across the country. Not all provinces have a mandated form that by law must be used. In Table 7, you will find the name and/or number of the form for your province, together with the name and/or number of any documents that go with it. You will find a blank sample of each document in the download that comes with this book. For the provinces that do not have a legally mandated form, I have included a form that is suitable for each province.

You will see that each province and territory refers to a schedule, scale, or tariff. These are also noted in Table 7. The schedule or tariff is a list of possible actions that you took as part of your lawsuit, such as filing an affidavit or participating in an examination or spending a day in court. Each item has a dollar amount attached to it; the dollar amount is the sum you are allowed to claim for having paid your lawyer to take that step.

To calculate your Bill of Costs, you must first look at the schedule or tariff to see which items apply to you, then put those items on your Bill of Costs with the accompanying dollar amount. You will then add up the items to come to a total of the amount you may claim. Note that the fee items may only be claimed if you paid a lawyer to handle them for you, while the expenses may be claimed whether or not you worked with a lawyer.

There are more detailed instructions in the accompanying download for the different provinces. The tariffs and schedules themselves are also included in your download. If there is a step you took that is not listed on the schedule or tariff, then you are not allowed to claim anything for that step.

After you have completed your Bill of Costs, you will send a copy of it (without receipts or other attachments) to the person who has been ordered to pay your costs. If that person had a lawyer representing him or her in court, send it to the lawyer and not directly to the person. If that person agrees that you have properly prepared your Bill of Costs and that you have not claimed anything inappropriate, he or she will make arrangements to pay it.

The different provinces have somewhat different procedures for getting a matter to the assessment officer. Make sure you follow the specific directions for your province or territory in the accompanying download materials.

7. Can the Other Side Get Costs against Me?

As discussed earlier in this book, the general rule of costs is that the loser of the lawsuit may pay for the costs of the winner. Therefore, if you should lose your lawsuit or a significant part of it, the judge may order costs against you. This means you would have to

TABLE 7
BILL OF COSTS

Province or Territory	Form	Also Attach	Where to Find More Information in the Rules of Court
Alberta	Form 44	• Receipts for out-of-pocket expenses • Copy of the order that awards costs to you	Rule 10.35 of the Rules of Court
British Columbia	Form 62	• Receipts for out-of-pocket expenses • Copy of the order that awards costs to you	Rule 57 (28)
Manitoba	Form 58C	• Receipts for out-of-pocket expenses • Copy of the order that awards costs to you	Rule 58
New Brunswick	No form mandated	• Form 59A Notice of Appointment to Assess Costs • Receipts for out-of-pocket expenses • Copy of the order that awards costs to you	Rule 59
Newfoundland and Labrador	No form mandated	• Receipts for out-of-pocket expenses • Copy of the order that awards costs to you	Rule 55 Regulation 45/11 Column 3
Northwest Territories	No form mandated	• Receipts for out-of-pocket expenses • Copy of the order that awards costs to you	Rules of Court Part 50 Rule 648 Column 3 of Schedule A
Nova Scotia	No form mandated	• Receipts for out-of-pocket expenses • Copy of the order that awards costs to you	Rule 77.06 Tariff C through E
Nunavut	No form mandated	• Receipts for out-of-pocket expenses • Copy of the order that awards costs to you	Rules of Court, part 50 Rule 648 Column 3 of Schedule A
Ontario	Form 57A	• Receipts for out-of-pocket expenses • Copy of the order that awards costs to you	Tariff A

TABLE 7 — CONTINUED

Prince Edward Island	Form 58B	• Receipts for out-of-pocket expenses • Copy of the order that awards costs to you	Rule 58 subrule 57.01(1) and the Tariffs
Saskatchewan	Form 11-13B	• Receipts for out-of-pocket expenses • Copy of the order that awards costs to you	Schedule I
Yukon	Form 68 unless it's an order under R 17 (costs payable from an estate), then use form 69	• Receipts for out-of-pocket expenses • Copy of the order that awards costs to you	Rule 60

pay the legal costs of other parties according to the Bill of Costs they provide. With litigation, there is never a guarantee that you will win and there is never a guarantee that even if you win, you will get your costs paid by the other party.

14
Alternatives to Court Battles

Though every lawsuit is different, there is a strict procedure that governs how the lawsuit is carried out. There are also tried and true methods and steps that may help you move your legal matter ahead before you get to court, to end proceedings that are already underway, or perhaps even to settle your issues completely without going to court at all.

You should look at going to court as a last resort, to be used only when all other methods of resolving the issues have failed. This is partly because court battles are lengthy, stressful, and use up a lot of personal and public resources. It is also partly because the court expects responsible adults to be able to resolve most matters amongst themselves and only ask for help when they really need it.

This chapter covers some of the things that happen outside the courtroom either before court or instead of going to court. You may find that one or more of these activities will help you resolve your lawsuit without a trial.

1. Are There Alternatives to Fighting It out in Court?

Although this book is about launching a court battle, it makes sense to talk about the alternatives to court fights. As has been mentioned in this book, getting your lawsuit all the way to a trial can take years. It takes a thick skin and a tolerance for stress. It may also take a lot of money as well as time away from work and other activities. It is always a good idea to consider other means of settling your issue. At best, you'll resolve the matter without the time and money it would have taken to fight it out. At worst, you'll still end up going to court, which you were prepared to do in any event.

Sometimes a settlement may take place without the lawsuit actually having been started, simply because the opposing parties were able to agree on the key issues. That would be ideal, since it would cost little money and take little time. This is where the demand letter comes in, (described in section 2.), as do some other methods described in this chapter. However, keep in mind that even if you have begun suing an estate, you may propose a settlement at any time. The fact that you have an upcoming court date or are in the middle of discoveries does not in any way prevent you from presenting the other side with an offer. When offers of settlement are sent "without prejudice," the judge will not be told about the offer.

Note that there are some matters that you cannot settle between the parties. Some require the court's assistance no matter what. For example, where the executor is asking the court to interpret words or phrases in a will, it makes no difference whether other parties agree on what the words mean. The judge is the only person who can legally make that call. The position of the various parties will be considered by the judge but it is not a deciding factor.

2. Demand Letter

Every lawsuit should be preceded by a demand letter. This is a letter to the person you intend to sue that tells him or her what you are going to sue about and gives you both a chance to settle it before you go to court. The letter is intended to accomplish a few goals, all of which may help you resolve your dispute. See Chapter 1, section 6. for more about when and how to draft a demand letter.

3. Negotiations

As mentioned in section 2., your demand letter is intended to state your position and elicit a reply from the other party that states his or her position. Ideally, this may be the beginning of a negotiation. Negotiating simply means that you and the other person (or his or her lawyer) will write or call back and forth to each other to discuss the situation,

make offers and counter-offers, and hopefully come up with a solution that both of you can live with. Certainly not all negotiations are successful and in some cases you may not even have the chance to begin negotiations, but you can make this stage of the proceedings work well for you if you handle it properly.

First, figure out your goals and prioritize them. This is not something you would show to the person on the other side of the dispute, but it is an essential tool for you. Are there parts of your argument or situation that are simply so important that you cannot and will not give them up? Are there other parts of the situation that are important, but you could live without them? In other words, know which things you are willing to compromise about and which ones are simply nonnegotiable. For example, if you and your siblings are arguing about which items belonging to your parents should be given to which people, what is the one item that would top your list? Would you be willing to give up one or two things lower on the list if you could definitely get your number one item?

Negotiation involves some give and take. Certainly you are making a demand about what you want, but the person on the other side wants something too. Usually the two positions are diametrically opposed or you wouldn't be in the position of suing each other in the first place. The idea of the negotiation is for each party to compromise so that both sides come away with something that might not be ideal, but is better than carrying on the fight. Each side will win part of what they wanted.

In negotiations, both sides will try to show how the law supports their position. They try to point out the weaknesses in the other side's case. This is because underlying the negotiations is the knowledge that if it doesn't work, the parties are going to proceed to court and they are each going to do whatever it takes to win. Each wants to show the other that the law is on their side and therefore they have a good likelihood of succeeding in court. Because of this sort of tone, negotiations are not friendly. In fact, sometimes they seem awfully close to threatening. Make sure you do not step over the line into threats against the other parties.

4. Without Prejudice

Negotiations are generally done in writing. Whenever you write to the people on the other side or their lawyer to say anything at all — no matter how small — about your case, you should put the words "without prejudice" prominently across the top of the letter. It is usually inserted right below the date and right above the address or name of the person to whom you are writing.

The purpose of using this phrase is to keep your proposed concessions out of court so that they cannot be used against you. Imagine, for example, that you are asking for the deceased's home to be transferred to you on the basis of resulting trust. Your position in court is that the house should be yours and that you do not want money or anything else as a substitute. In the spirit of negotiation, you might write a letter to the other side saying that they can keep the house and pay you $400,000 and that would be the end of it. You do not want them to show up in court saying that at one point you were willing to give up the house because that might weaken your case.

In the legal world, the word "prejudice" means legal harm. It refers to something that weakens or jeopardizes your legal rights or position. When correspondence has been marked "without prejudice," the other side cannot ever use it in court or put it into an affidavit or in any way use its contents in court against you. This works both ways of course; you cannot use anyone else's "without prejudice" correspondence against them, either. It is fair for both sides to say to a judge in court that everyone has tried to come to an agreement but they weren't able to do so. However, no more detail than that can be given.

If someone does try to use your "without prejudice" documents or letters against you in court, you should object to that in court. Ask the judge to throw out the document that contains your "without prejudice" paperwork.

Remember that email messages count as written messages and their contents could be used against you. They must also be marked as being "without prejudice."

5. Mediation

Mediation is the process of meeting with the person or people with whom you have a dispute along with a trained, neutral person who will guide your discussions.

The idea of mediation is for everyone involved to focus on how they are going to resolve things. Never mind who started it or how badly people have been behaving. All of you have to ignore that and move forward. Both sides have to be interested in ending the battle as opposed to winning the battle. Everyone has to try to listen to the other side. Both sides will get a chance to speak and both sides will have control over whether or not they agree to any proposed settlement. Similar to negotiating, everyone is likely going to have to compromise on some issue or point, but unlike negotiating, the process is cooperative.

Many estate disputes can be mediated. The following are some examples:

1. A parent's will leaves all of the personal items to the adult children, but they cannot agree on how to divide them.

2. One child is left out of the will. Some of the siblings want to share the estate evenly, including the child who was left out, while others don't.

3. An executor wants to claim compensation for his or her work on the estate, but the beneficiaries think he or she is asking for too much money.

4. A parent's will left the cabin to all of her children jointly, but the children who live in another province don't want to pay their share of expenses for a cabin they don't use.

5. An executor won't provide the information or records the beneficiaries want to see.

6. After the death of a parent, the executor, who is one of the kids, has let one of his children live rent-free in the house and drive the deceased's vehicle, all against the wishes of the beneficiaries.

7. Some of the children believe that one child received the bulk of a parent's estate because he or she unduly influenced the parent.

In a mediation session, there is no judge involved. There is no arbitrator who will hand down a binding decision. Some mediations involve lawyers representing the parties but many do not. The mediator is neutral, and aims to reach an agreement that everyone can live with. There is no risk of having anything imposed on you during mediation because you always have the ability to say no to any given proposal or suggestion. As long as everyone who participates does so with the mindset of cooperation rather than aggression, the session stands an excellent chance of resulting in an agreement that suits everyone.

In most mediations, the parties will agree on who is to act as mediator to ensure that the person who is chosen is neutral and has no prior connection to any of the parties. The mediator is often a lawyer who has knowledge of estate matters because this will speed the process and improve your chances of reaching an agreement that stays fully within the parameters of what is allowable in estate law. There are plenty of professional, trained mediators in most cities.

Mediation can be wrapped up much more quickly than a court battle. Whereas it may take years to get a matter to trial, a mediation session can take place within a few weeks. There is some preparation work to be done first; each party will send a written summary to the mediator so that he or she can become familiar with the estate and the parties' respective positions. This also helps narrow down the number of topics to be discussed.

A factor that many participants in mediation appreciate is that it protects the privacy of all involved. There is no court record for outside people to see. The mediator's notes are never allowed to be seen in court and in fact are destroyed after an agreement is reached. This is done so that everyone may speak freely and toss around ideas without wondering whether their suggestions will later be held against them. If the session is successful, there may be an order drawn up by the mediator that people can sign right there and then. Even if not all of the issues are resolved, mediation is considered successful if some important matters are resolved.

Because mediation is not about blame, there are no accusations or pointing fingers.

In fact, the mediator will not allow individuals to do that in a mediation session. There are rules about how people must behave in order that the session may progress.

One of the saddest aspects of any estate battle is that it pits family members against each other and destroys family relationships. Many families never recover from it. With mediation, the focus is about working together. Everyone goes into the session knowing full well the parties do not agree on everything. They know there is a serious issue, but they have enough respect for each other to prefer to settle it and remain a family than sue each other.

Meditation also costs only a fraction of what a trial would cost. The cost of hiring the mediator is shared among all of the parties to the mediation.

Though mediation is an extremely useful tool in estate disputes, it is not for everyone. If you are afraid for your safety in the presence of a specific person, it is not a good idea to sit face-to-face with that person to try to resolve an argument. You do not want to risk injury or emotional trauma. Even when physical safety is not an issue, some people are so bitter and angry that it would be overwhelmingly upsetting to spend time in the same room, not to mention pointless. Mediation is only going to work if everyone is able to stay reasonably calm and feel free to speak up.